38

STUDY GUIDE

America, 1840–1895: Expansion and Consolidation

AQA - GCSE

Published by Clever Lili Limited.

contact@cleverlili.com

First published 2020

ISBN 978-1-913887-37-7

Cover by: Acrogame on Adobe Stock

Icons by: flaticon and freepik

Contributors: James George, Muirin Gillespie-Gallery, Emily Bishop, Marcus Pailing, Shahan Abu Shumel Haydar, Rebecca Lawrence

Edited by Paul Connolly and Rebecca Parsley

Design by Evgeni Veskov and Will Fox

Contents

HOW TO USE THIS BOOK

In this study guide, you will see a series of icons, highlighted words and page references. The key below will help you quickly establish what these mean and where to go for more information.

Icons

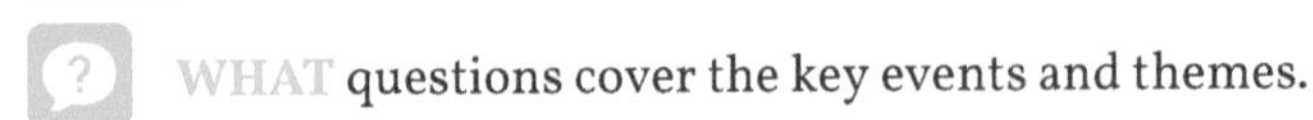

WHAT questions cover the key events and themes.

WHO questions cover the key people involved.

WHEN questions cover the timings of key events.

WHERE questions cover the locations of key moments.

WHY questions cover the reasons behind key events.

HOW questions take a closer look at the way in which events, situations and trends occur.

IMPORTANCE questions take a closer look at the significance of events, situations, and recurrent trends and themes.

DECISIONS questions take a closer look at choices made at events and situations during this era.

Highlighted words

Abdicate - occasionally, you will see certain words highlighted within an answer. This means that, if you need it, you'll find an explanation of the word or phrase in the glossary which starts on **page 71**.

Page references

Tudor *(p.7)* - occasionally, a certain subject within an answer is covered in more depth on a different page. If you'd like to learn more about it, you can go directly to the page indicated.

America, 1840-1895: Expansion and Consolidation, is a period study that investigates two aspects of the history of the United States in the second half of the nineteenth century. 'Expansion' explores the move westwards by settlers and pioneers, and the ensuing conflicts with Native American peoples. 'Consolidation' refers to the forging of the United States as a nation, through its political and economic growth. You will study a range of significant events, people and situations, which shaped the United States throughout this period.

Purpose

This study enables you to understand the challenges facing the United States, and how it overcame them. The challenges ranged from political conflict between the federal government and individual states, to the social and moral issues of dealing with slavery and Native American culture. Through the study of this topic you will develop key historical skills, such as cause and consequence, and change and continuity. You will also be encouraged to develop your critical thinking skills, through the analysis of interpretations.

Enquiries

America, 1840-1895: Expansion and Consolidation features 3 key enquiry topics:

- Enquiry 1 looks at the American West, exploring the lifestyles of the Native Americans who lived on the Great Plains. It also examines the opportunities it offered for settlement, and studies the people who tried to carve their lives out of the Great American Desert.
- Enquiry 2 focuses on the growing conflicts in the United States at this time: the wars between the US Government and the Native Americans of the Great Plains, and the internal struggle between northern and southern states in the American Civil War.
- Finally. Enquiry 3 explores how conflict was overcome. It looks at reconciliation and reconstruction in the aftermath of the Civil War. It then examines the fate of Native Americans, the permanent settlement of the American West, and the end of the Indian Frontier.

Key Individuals

Some of the key individuals studied on this course include:

- Brigham Young.
- Little Crow.
- Red Cloud.
- Abraham Lincoln.
- Crazy Horse.
- Sitting Bull.
- George Armstrong Custer.

Key Events

Some of the key events you will study on this course include:

- The California Gold Rush.
- The Indian Wars.
- The American Civil War.
- The abolition of slavery.
- The Battle of the Little Bighorn.

Assessment

America, 1840-1895: Expansion and Consolidation is the period study component of your AQA qualification. It is examined in Paper 1. You should spend 1 hour on this section of the paper. There will be 6 exam questions: in questions 1-3 you will be required to assess and evaluate two historical interpretations about the period using detailed contextual knowledge. Questions 4-6 are purely knowledge based.

- Question 1 is worth 4 marks. This question requires you to describe and explain how two interpretations are different.
- Question 2 is worth 4 marks. This question requires you to describe and explain why the two interpretations are different.

- Question 3 is worth 8 marks. This question requires you to explain how convincing the interpretations are. You must give a substantiated judgement, based on the interpretations and your contextual knowledge.
- Question 4 is worth 4 marks. This is a 'describe' question, in which you must provide two detailed reasons/examples/features about a particular topic covered in America, 1840-1895.
- Question 5 is worth 8 marks. This question will test your understanding of second order concepts (cause, consequence, change, continuity, etc.). In this question you must demonstrate your knowledge about a topic you have covered, and give different reasons based on the second order concept you are given.
- Question 6 is worth 12 marks. This question will ask you to pick between two events, individuals or situations, an will ask you to make a sustained judgement of both bullet points, using your contextual knowledge and understanding of second order concepts.

Revision! A dreaded word. Everyone knows it's coming, everyone knows how much it helps with your exam performance, and everyone struggles to get started! We know you want to do the best you can in your GCSEs, but schools aren't always clear on the best way to revise. This can leave students wondering:

✓ How should I plan my revision time?
✓ How can I beat procrastination?
✓ What methods should I use? Flash cards? Re-reading my notes? Highlighting?

Luckily, you no longer need to guess at the answers. Education researchers have looked at all the available revision studies, and the jury is in. They've come up with some key pointers on the best ways to revise, as well as some thoughts on popular revision methods that aren't so helpful. The next few pages will help you understand what we know about the best revision methods.

How can I beat procrastination?

This is an age-old question, and it applies to adults as well! Have a look at our top three tips below.

Reward yourself

When we think a task we have to do is going to be boring, hard or uncomfortable, we often put if off and do something more 'fun' instead. But we often don't really enjoy the 'fun' activity because we feel guilty about avoiding what we should be doing. Instead, get your work done and promise yourself a reward after you complete it. Whatever treat you choose will seem all the sweeter, and you'll feel proud for doing something you found difficult. Just do it!

Just do it!

We tend to procrastinate when we think the task we have to do is going to be difficult or dull. The funny thing is, the most uncomfortable part is usually making ourselves sit down and start it in the first place. Once you begin, it's usually not nearly as bad as you anticipated.

Pomodoro technique

The pomodoro technique helps you trick your brain by telling it you only have to focus for a short time. Set a timer for 20 minutes and focus that whole period on your revision. Turn off your phone, clear your desk, and work. At the end of the 20 minutes, you get to take a break for five. Then, do another 20 minutes. You'll usually find your rhythm and it becomes easier to carry on because it's only for a short, defined chunk of time.

Spaced practice

We tend to arrange our revision into big blocks. For example, you might tell yourself: "This week I'll do all my revision for the Cold War, then next week I'll do the Medicine Through Time unit."

This is called **massed practice**, because all revision for a single topic is done as one big mass.

But there's a better way! Try **spaced practice** instead. Instead of putting all revision sessions for one topic into a single block, space them out. See the example below for how it works.

This means planning ahead, rather than leaving revision to the last minute - but the evidence strongly suggests it's worth it. You'll remember much more from your revision if you use **spaced practice** rather than organising it into big blocks. Whichever method you choose, though, remember to reward yourself with breaks.

Spaced practice (more effective):

week 1	week 2	week 3	week 4
Topic 1	Topic 1	Topic 1	Topic 1
Topic 2	Topic 2	Topic 2	Topic 2
Topic 3	Topic 3	Topic 3	Topic 3
Topic 4	Topic 4	Topic 4	Topic 4

Massed practice (less effective)

week 1	week 2	week 3	week 4
Topic 1	Topic 2	Topic 3	Topic 4

What methods should I use to revise?

Self-testing/flash cards

Self explanation/mind-mapping

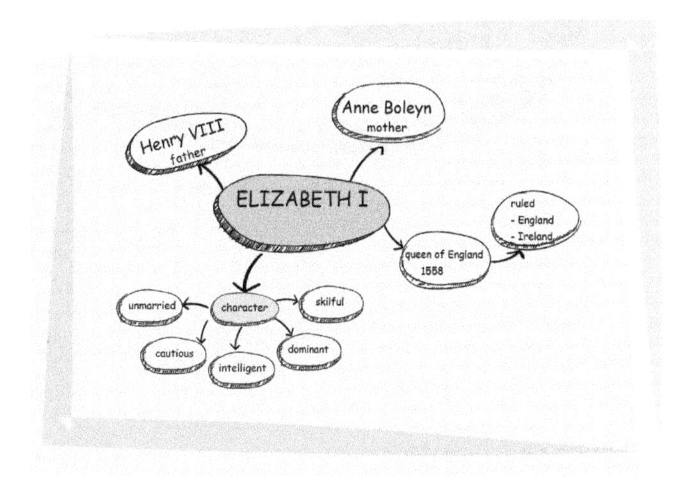

The research shows a clear winner for revision methods - **self-testing.** A good way to do this is with **flash cards.** Flash cards are really useful for helping you recall short – but important – pieces of information, like names and dates.

Side A - question

Side B - answer

Write questions on one side of the cards, and the answers on the back. This makes answering the questions and then testing yourself easy. Put all the cards you get right in a pile to one side, and only repeat the test with the ones you got wrong - this will force you to work on your weaker areas.

pile with right answers

pile with wrong answers

As this book has a quiz question structure itself, you can use it for this technique.

Another good revision method is **self-explanation.** This is where you explain how and why one piece of information from your course linked with another piece.

This can be done with **mind-maps**, where you draw the links and then write explanations for how they connect. For example, President Truman is connected with anti-communism because of the Truman Doctrine.

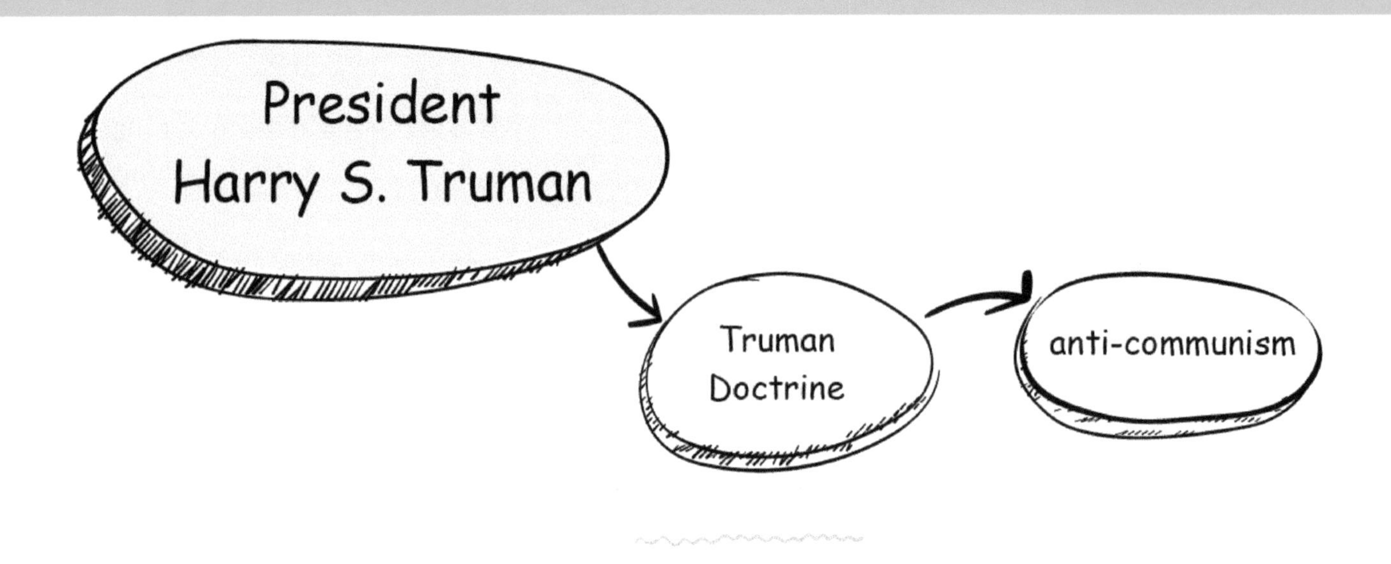

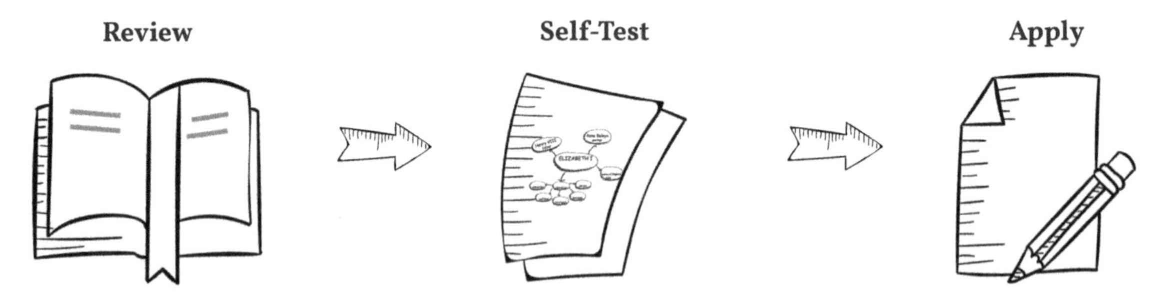

Start by highlighting or re-reading to create your flashcards for self-testing.

Test yourself with flash cards. Make mind maps to explain the concepts.

Apply your knowledge on practice exam questions.

Which revision techniques should I be cautious about?

Highlighting and **re-reading** are not necessarily bad strategies - but the research does say they're less effective than flash cards and mind-maps.

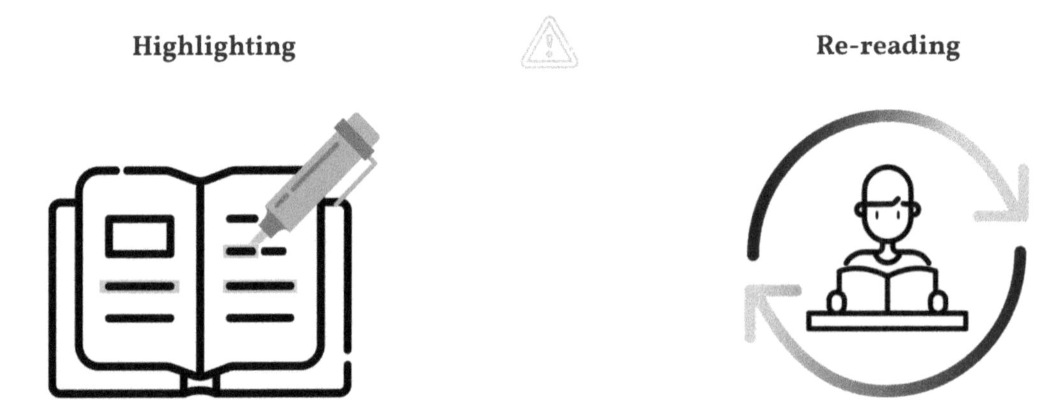

If you do use these methods, make sure they are **the first step to creating flash cards**. Really engage with the materia as you go, rather than switching to autopilot.

TIMELINE
1820
Missouri Compromise (p.40)
1830
1830s - Pioneer farmers began to move west (p.20)
April - Church of Jesus Christ of the Latter-day Saints (Mormons) founded (p.22)
May - Indian Removal Act established the Permanent Indian Frontier (p.31)
1831
Nat Turner's rebellion (p.40)
1833
Anti-Slavery Society established (p.41)
1836
First wagon train successfully used the Oregon Trail (p.18)
1845
Term 'Manifest Destiny' first used (p.17)
1846
Donner Party (p.20)
1847
July - Jenner published his findings 'An Enquiry into the Causes and Effects of the Variolae Vaccinae'
1849
1849-1852 - California Gold Rush (p.22)
1850
Compromise of 1850 (p.41)
1850 - Fugitive Slave Act (p.42)
1851
March - First Indian Appropriations Act established reservations (p.32)
September - First Fort Laramie Treaty (p.33)
1854
May - Kansas-Nebraska Act (p.43)
August - Sioux Wars began (p.35)
1854-1861 - Bleeding Kansas (p.43)
1857
Mountain Meadows Massacre (p.49)
1859
October - Harper's Ferry raid (p.44)
1860
December - South Carolina seceded from the USA. Other states followed in 1861 (p.46)
1861
April - American Civil War began (p.47)
1862
Homestead Act (p.56)

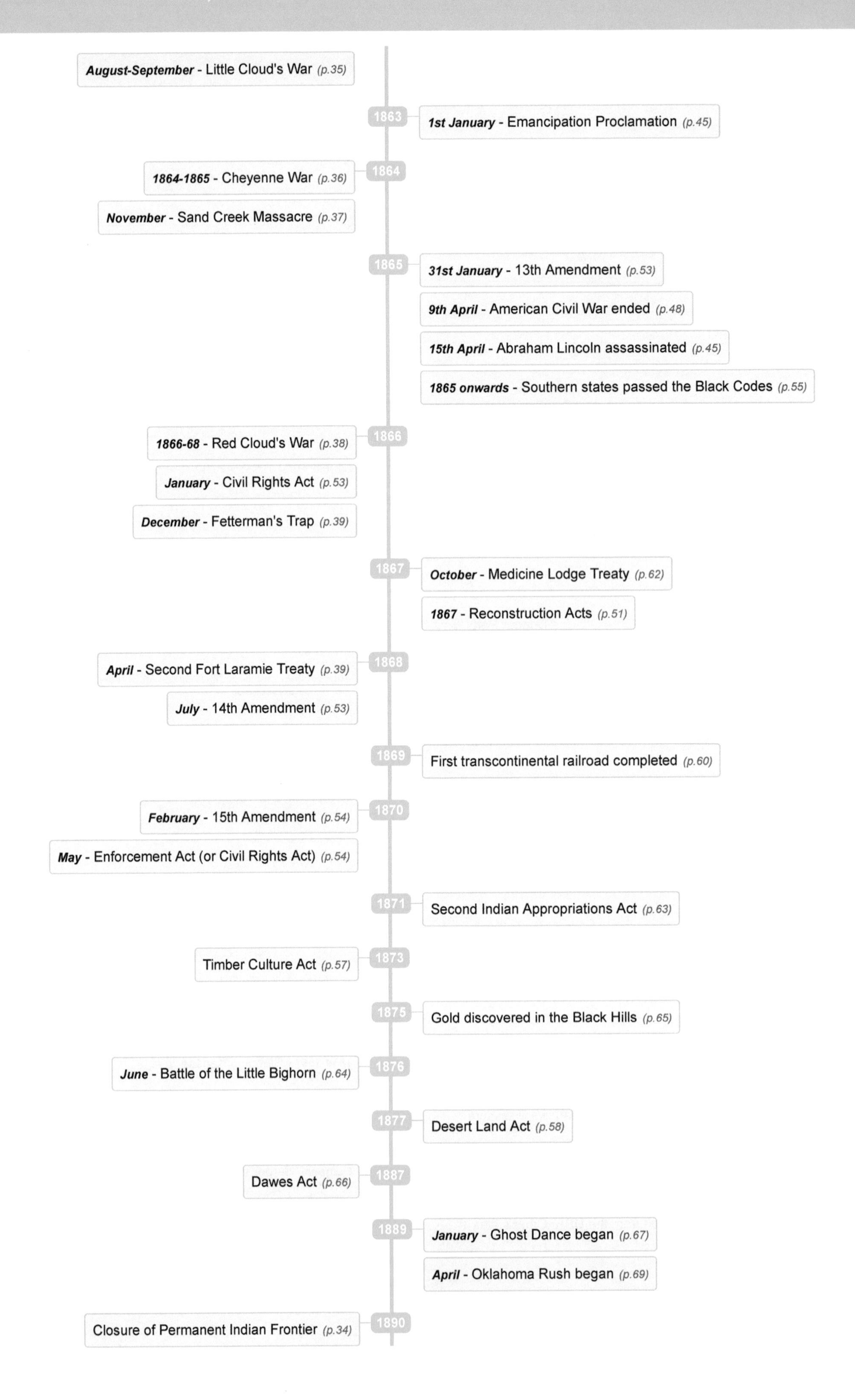
August-September - Little Cloud's War (p.35)
1863
1st January - Emancipation Proclamation (p.45)
1864
1864-1865 - Cheyenne War (p.36)
November - Sand Creek Massacre (p.37)
1865
31st January - 13th Amendment (p.53)
9th April - American Civil War ended (p.48)
15th April - Abraham Lincoln assassinated (p.45)
1865 onwards - Southern states passed the Black Codes (p.55)
1866
1866-68 - Red Cloud's War (p.38)
January - Civil Rights Act (p.53)
December - Fetterman's Trap (p.39)
1867
October - Medicine Lodge Treaty (p.62)
1867 - Reconstruction Acts (p.51)
1868
April - Second Fort Laramie Treaty (p.39)
July - 14th Amendment (p.53)
1869
First transcontinental railroad completed (p.60)
1870
February - 15th Amendment (p.54)
May - Enforcement Act (or Civil Rights Act) (p.54)
1871
Second Indian Appropriations Act (p.63)
1873
Timber Culture Act (p.57)
1875
Gold discovered in the Black Hills (p.65)
1876
June - Battle of the Little Bighorn (p.64)
1877
Desert Land Act (p.58)
1887
Dawes Act (p.66)
1889
January - Ghost Dance began (p.67)
April - Oklahoma Rush began (p.69)
1890
Closure of Permanent Indian Frontier (p.34)

December - Battle of Wounded Knee. Sioux Wars ended *(p.68)*

THE GREAT AMERICAN DESERT

The term used by people who lived east of the Mississippi River, when it was 'unknown' land.

What was the Great American Desert?

The Great American Desert was the area of land between the Mississippi River and the Rocky Mountains. This was the name given to the area by the early settlers in America - later it became known as the 'Great Plains'.

What did white settlers think of the Great American Desert?

Due to the poor conditions, the area now known as the Great Plains was dismissed by most Americans as inhospitable. They called it the Great American Desert.

Why was the Great American Desert inhospitable?

There were 3 reasons why the Great American Desert was thought to be difficult to live in.

- The weather was extreme. It was cold and windy in the winter, and hot and dry in the summer.
- A lack of natural resources, particularly wood, made it difficult to build a home or farm the land.
- Dangerous or disruptive animals, like wolves and locusts, could cause problems for settlers.
- There were huge thunderstorms. Lightning could ignite fires that raged through the dry grass.

How did native people survive in the American Desert?

Although white Americans struggled to survive on the Great Plains, Native Americans thrived. They had developed ways in which to survive its conditions, mainly focused on a nomadic way of life.

- The Native Americans followed the vast herds of buffalo *(p.28)*, which provided them with food and other resources. No part of a buffalo was wasted.
- They used tipis as homes, as these were easy to carry, and to erect and dismantle.
- They treated the land and animals with respect. This reverence helped them survive, as they co-existed with nature, and this honoured the Great Spirit.

How could native people survive the winter in the American Desert?

When the winter was particularly harsh the tribes sometimes moved into wooden lodges. These were circular buildings built from earth and logs, with a fire in the centre. They could fit around 60 people inside a lodge.

Why did attitudes towards the American Desert begin to change in the 1840s?

The USA won a war against Mexico in 1848. It took over land in California and Oregon. Texas also joined the Union in 1845. These two events meant that white settlers had to cross the American Desert to get to the new territories.

DID YOU KNOW?

At the time it was known as 'The Great American Desert', the area was only inhabited by Native American Indians. White settlers deemed it to be uninhabitable.

MANIFEST DESTINY

Destined to expand!

What was Manifest Destiny?

Manifest Destiny was the belief that white people had a God-given right to expand westwards, and to settle the entire continent of North America. It was also viewed by many as a mission to civilise the 'savage' Native American tribes.

Who thought of the concept of Manifest Destiny?

The journalist John L. O'Sullivan coined the phrase in 1845, to encourage people to travel west.

Why was Manifest Destiny important?

Manifest Destiny was important for 6 reasons.

- It increased the size of the United States, as more people moved westward.
- Americans gained access to new resources, such as gold, which made the economy grow.
- It caused major unrest in the Native American tribes.
- It opened up new land for settling, which led to laws such as the Homestead Act *(p.56)* of 1862.
- The idea that God wanted whites to settle the land made it easier for them to justify taking it from Native Americans.
- It was a major 'pull' factor in the expansion west.

How did the painting 'American Progress' show Manifest Destiny?

The painting 'American Progress' from 1872 shows the American ideals of Manifest Destiny. The painting shows the many types of migrants, including farmers and miners, and it shows a female representation of 'progress' as the Americans move across to the West. It shows the introduction of telegraph poles and the railroad. The Native Americans, the buffalo *(p.28)* herds, and wild animals are all being driven away by the white Americans.

DID YOU KNOW?

It was believed by many that God blessed the expansion of the American nation, and that He even demanded it.

THE OREGON TRAIL

A trail that was established to encourage settlers to move west.

What was the Oregon Trail?

The Oregon Trail was the route used by thousands of people to cross from the east, over the Great Plains, to the west. It was 3,200km long.

Where was the Oregon Trail?

The trail started in Independence, Missouri, and finished in Oregon City.

How did people travel on the Oregon Trail?

Pioneers travelled along the Oregon Trail by foot, horseback, or with wagons. They had to bring enough food for the entire journey, as well as the things they needed for their new life. Wagons were often pulled by oxen as they were strong, but they were very slow.

Why did people travel the Oregon Trail?

People wanted to move west, as they had heard of rich farming lands which they could obtain for free *(p.52)*. The economic conditions in the east were not good, so people saw it as a new opportunity.

At what time of year did people travel the Oregon Trail?

People were advised not to travel the Oregon Trail in winter, as it froze, and not to travel until April at the earliest. This would allow the grass to grow, so that their animals could graze along the route.

Why did settlers not use an alternative to the Oregon Trail?

People could travel by sea to Oregon, but it was extremely expensive. Each journey cost $300, and the journey could take a year. Taking the overland trail cost them the price of a wagon and supplies.

Who established the Oregon Trail?

Jedediah Smith established the Oregon Trail in 1825, when he discovered the South Pass through the Rocky Mountains.

Who were the first migrants with a wagon to use the Oregon Trail?

In 1836, two couples were the first to travel the Oregon Trail with a covered wagon for purposes other than trade. Narcissa and Marcus Whitman, and Henry and Eliza Spalding, were Christian missionaries.

What other examples of people travelling the Oregon Trail are there?

Once it was open, many groups used the Oregon Trail. It was safer to travel in groups with a range of skills. They formed 'wagon trains'.

- In 1840, the Walker family travelled the trail, with their 5 children.
- A group of 60 completed the trail in 1841, and another 100 in 1842.
- The 'Great Emigration' of 1843 saw Marcus Whitman leading 900 people along the trail.
- By 1846, an estimated 5,000 people had used the Oregon Trail to migrate west.

How did the government help people use the Oregon Trail?

The American government wanted people to use the Oregon Trail and move west, so they spent money on mapping and publishing reports on the trail. In 1841 the government spent $30,000 on promoting the trail.

What problems were there using the Oregon Trail?

There were many difficulties in travelling the Oregon Trail, and it is believed that around 20,000 people died on the trail, including the famous Donner Party *(p.20)*. The main problems were:

- Getting stuck.
- Drowning while crossing rivers.
- Accidents with wagons.
- Illness and disease, such as cholera.
- Running out of supplies.
- Fear of attack from Native Americans, although there are no recorded accounts of any.
- The length of the journey. The average journey on the Oregon Trail took four months.

DID YOU KNOW?

The trail was scattered with litter!

Many travellers would dump old wagons, clothes, food, and other rubbish.

MOUNTAIN MEN

Most had to report to someone.

Who were the mountain men?

Mountain men were hunters and trappers, who caught animals in the Rocky Mountains.

When did the mountain men go west?

They were the first pioneers to go west, from the early part of the nineteenth century.

What did the mountain men hunt?

They hunted animals for fur, such as deer, elk, beaver, and buffalo *(p.28)*.

What was life like for the mountain men?

They had a solitary life, but met every year at rendezvous points to trade their furs.

Why were the mountain men important?

They created the first trails that other settlers later used to move west. Sometimes, people paid them to lead them safely over the mountains.

DID YOU KNOW?

Most mountain men had to report to the head of their trapping party. This man was named a 'boosway': a version of the French word 'bourgeois'.

PIONEER FARMERS

A pioneer farmer could get rich.

Who were the pioneer farmers?

Pioneer farmers were the first farmers to travel west, to Oregon and California.

When did the pioneer farmers go west?

People travelled west from the 1830s. They are known as the pioneer farmers.

Why did the pioneer farmers go west?

The pioneer farmers travelled west for 4 main reasons.

- They wanted independence.
- There was a financial crisis in the eastern states, which in 1837 led to 25% unemployment. Wages were cut by 40%.
- The east was becoming overpopulated.
- There was cheap farming land to claim, giving the pioneers a home and employment.
- There was a huge demand for food, so they could make a lot of money through farming, and by exporting any excess to Europe.

How did the pioneer farmers farm?

Larger farms could use steam-powered machinery, and retain a larger labour force of people.

DID YOU KNOW?

Some farmers could improve the land they bought, and then sell it for far more than they paid for it. They then moved further west, bought more land, and repeated the process.

THE DONNER PARTY

A group of pioneers had a dream to go west. They ended up facing terrible winter conditions, and had to make disturbing decisions to stay alive.

Who were the Donner Party?

The Donner Party were travellers from the east, on their way to California. They were led by the Donner brothers, using a new shorter trail mapped by Lansford Hastings. They became trapped in the mountains during the winter, and turned to cannibalism to survive.

When did the Donner Party travel to California?

The Donner Party started their journey in May 1846, but became trapped in the winter of 1846. The first person died on the 15th December.

How many people were in the Donner Party?

87 people left for California, but only 46 arrived.

Why did the Donner Party get stranded?

The Donner Party became stranded for several reasons.

- They left later than other pioneers that year.
- They took a new and more difficult route, which was meant to be shorter. However, it was away from the more common trails, so was harder to follow.
- The weather was poor, and the winter was particularly harsh. Snow storms trapped them in the mountains.
- Because the route was not established it had no forts where they could get supplies. There were also no established river crossings. These had to be created from scratch, which made the journey harder.

DID YOU KNOW?

It was said that the survivors did not kill anyone to eat ... except for two people.

- ✓ Two Native Americans, Luis and Salvador from the Miwok tribe, were sent to help the trapped pioneers. They eventually became trapped themselves.
- ✓ When they had eaten the pioneers who died, it was decided that the Miwoks would be killed and eaten. They were seen as not 'really human'.

MINERS

Pioneers who wanted to get their hands on the precious metals that had been discovered in California.

Who were the miners?

Miners were pioneers who travelled west to pan for precious metals, such as gold.

Why did the miners go west?

Gold was discovered at Sutter's Fort, California. This led to a rush of miners to the area in 1849 - hence their nickname, 'forty-niners'.

Where did the miners come from?

Initially the miners came from the eastern states of the US but, as word spread, they came from Europe and Asia too.

What was life like for miners?

Life in the mining camps was hard, with long, hot days and uncomfortable nights in temporary shelters. Many men did not make enough money to stay long and went home empty-handed.

What was the impact of miners on the Native American population?

Miners, and the towns that grew up around the gold rush *(p.22)*, took land and resources from the Native Americans. Their movement disturbed the buffalo *(p.28)*. The people also brought diseases the Native Americans had not experienced before, meaning they experienced high fatality rates. All this led to conflict and wars, such as Red Cloud's War *(p.38)*.

DID YOU KNOW?

151,000 Chinese immigrants came to USA in search of a better life. Some wanted to take advantage of the discovery of precious metals.

- ✓ They became the largest non-white community from outside the US.
- ✓ However, they were viewed as 'competition' by other pioneers, as they often worked for lower wages.
- ✓ This led to the Chinese Exclusion Act in 1882. This led to a long period of poor treatment of Chinese and other Asian groups in the USA.

THE CALIFORNIA GOLD RUSH

The miners would scoop up the sand, rock and gravel and mix it with water to find precious metals, hoping for gold.

What was the California Gold Rush?

The California Gold Rush refers to the time when a huge wave of prospectors moved to California, to mine for gold.

When was the California Gold Rush?

Gold was first discovered in California in 1848. The California Gold Rush started in 1849.

Who discovered gold in California that started the Gold Rush?

James W. Marshall was the first to discover gold, at Sutter's Fort in California.

How many miners went west for the Gold Rush?

By April 1849, over 200,000 miners had travelled west.

What were the effects of the Gold Rush?

There were 6 consequences of the California Gold Rush.

- The American economy received a boost, which solved previous economic problems.
- California grew rapidly, becoming an official state in 1850. By 1855, the population in California was over 300,000.
- Huge farms and other businesses sprang up in California, making it a wealthy state where independance and wealth could be made. Farmers even started to export excess food around the world,
- The California Gold Rush was used as proof to some that Manifest Destiny was real.
- Problems with Native Americans on the trails to California increased.
- Mining camps were lawless places, where murder, claim jumping, racism, and assault were common.
- The wealth of the state was used in 1869 to pay for the first transcontinental railroad *(p.60)*.
- There were racial tensions with Chinese miners.

DID YOU KNOW?

The California Gold Rush attracted around 300,000 people from all over the world.

JOSEPH SMITH

Joseph Smith Jr. was the founder of Mormonism and the Latter-day Saints movement.

Who was Joseph Smith?

Joseph Smith was the founder and leader of The Church of Jesus Christ of Latter-Day Saints, otherwise known as the Mormons *(p.23)*.

When did Joseph Smith found Mormonism?

Joseph Smith founded the Church of Jesus Christ of Latter-Day Saints in 1830.

Why did Joseph Smith found the Mormon Church?

Joseph Smith believed the angel Moroni visited him and gave him a book from God, with instructions to share it with everyone.

When did Joseph Smith die?

There were a number of attempts to imprison Smith, but he managed to avoid them. Eventually he was imprisoned and, while there, he was killed by a mob.

Why was Joseph Smith important?

Joseph Smith was important because he created a new form of Christianity. He was persuasive and charismatic, so people followed him.

DID YOU KNOW?

He liked dogs!

He owned two dogs, one named Major and a bulldog named Baker.

BRIGHAM YOUNG

The second president of The Church of Jesus Christ of Latter-day Saints.

Who was Brigham Young?

Brigham Young was the president of the Church of Jesus Christ of the Latter-day Saints, or Mormons *(p.23)*, from 1844-1877.

Why is Brigham Young important?

Brigham Young was responsible for planning the Mormons *(p.23)*' journey to the Great Salt Lake *(p.25)*.

DID YOU KNOW?

Brigham Young founded Salt Lake City, and was the first Governor of Utah Territory.

PERSECUTION OF THE MORMONS IN THE EAST

A religious group that believes in revelations made by their founder Joseph Smith, as well as traditional concepts of Christianity.

What are Mormons?

Mormons are members of the Church of Jesus Christ of Latter-Day Saints.

Why were the Mormons important?

The Mormons are an example of how people were able to successfully travel and settle in the west.

Who was the leader of the Mormons?

Joseph Smith *(p.22)* was the founder and first leader of the Mormons.

Why were the Mormons persecuted?

There are 7 reasons why the Mormons faced persecution in the east by white Americans.

- The Mormons expanded rapidly, leading people to fear they were trying to take over.
- The Mormons moved into their own communities, which made people fearful of them. In 1833, the Mormons' printing press was destroyed in Independence, Missouri.
- The Mormons had a militia group called the Danites, who clashed with non-Mormons at the Battle of Crooked River in 1838.
- There was a financial crash in the 1830s, and people blamed the Mormons.
- In Nauvoo, the Mormons announced that they practised polygamy, which was against the Christian beliefs of most Americans. Many Americans thought that this was blasphemy.
- The Mormons encouraged the freeing of slaves, which went against the beliefs of most people in the southern states. This belief saw them forced out of Missouri.
- Americans were genuinely worried that Joseph Smith *(p.22)* was trying to overthrow the United States government.

When did the Mormons go west?

Brigham Young *(p.23)* moved all of the Mormons west in 1846-1847.

Where did the Mormons travel to?

The Mormons moved west to the Great Salt Lake (now in the state of Utah).

When did the Mormons reach Salt Lake?

The Mormons reached the Great Salt Lake in July 1847.

How did the Mormons organise the journey to Salt Lake?

The president of the Mormon church, Brigham Young *(p.23)*, carefully planned the journey. It was organised in 6 main ways.

- 16,000 people were formed into groups of 100 wagons, each with a leader.
- Each member of the group had a job and a purpose.
- Young researched the journey thoroughly.
- Young ensured discipline was tight.
- Young organised the Mormons at the Camp of Israel, ensuring that they reached the previously built Winter Quarters by autumn.
- A pioneer band of 143 strong people was sent ahead to the Great Salt Lake, to clear and ready the route, and to prepare a site for settlement.

What problems did the Mormons face on their journey west?

The Mormons faced 3 main problems on their journey.

- It was long - more than 1,000 miles.
- The weather was unpredictable.

- They didn't know what they'd find when they reached their destination.

In what ways were the Mormons successful at Salt Lake?

The Mormons successfully settled at the Great Salt Lake. There are 8 reasons for this success.

- Their leader, Brigham Young *(p.23)*, was highly respected and a brilliant organiser.
- They used irrigation systems to divert water from the mountains into the dry land around the Great Salt Lake.
- They used sod (mud) bricks to make houses, as wood was in short supply.
- Brigham Young *(p.23)* told the Mormons that all land was owned by the Church. He shared out the land according to need, so the bigger families had more land.
- When the Mormons first arrived at the Great Salt Lake it was part of Mexico. Brigham Young *(p.23)* negotiated with the US government, who incorporated it into the United States, calling the territory Utah from 1850.
- The Mormons charged travellers for the right to cross their land, which boosted their economy.
- Settlements were carefully organised. Each family was given a different task, so that the whole area could be self-sufficient.
- They encouraged people to come to the Great Salt Lake from all around the world, by creating the Perpetual Emigrating Fund. This meant that money could be given to emigrants to pay for their journey to America.

What is the significance of Salt Lake to the Mormons?

Salt Lake is the area where the Mormons settled after their journey west. It is now in the American state of Utah. Salt Lake City is the current headquarters of the Mormon Church.

DID YOU KNOW?

They have a lot of money!

Today, the Church's assets are thought to be worth more than $30 billion.

NATIVE AMERICANS

A group of peoples that had, and still have, an extraordinarily rich culture and way of living, that they have followed for thousands of years.

Who were the Native Americans?

Native Americans were the first peoples to live on the American continent. They were already living diverse, successful lives when the first Europeans arrived in the seventeenth century.

How many Native American tribes were there?

There were over 500 tribes. Those that lived on the Great Plains included the Sioux, the Apache, the Pawnee, and the Cheyenne.

What did Native Americans believe about the land?

The Native Americans believed the land was sacred, and often called it 'mother'. They believed it was a living thing, and they wanted to live in harmony with the land. They believed that no-one could own the land, and most tribes believed it should not be disturbed for farming.

- An example of the Native American respect for the land is the Lakota Sioux, who saw the Paha Sapa (Black Hills of South Dakota) as particularly sacred. They believed that their tribe originated in its caves.

What were some of the Native Americans' religious beliefs?

The Native Americans had some specific religious beliefs.

- They thought that spirits could guide them through 'vision quests'. Boys received a spirit animal when they reached puberty.
- They believed they could enter the spirit world by performing dances.
- Some personal items were 'charged' with spirits. Wearing these would bring luck or protection.

Why were circles important to Native Americans?

Circles were sacred to Native Americans, who believed they have spiritual significance. They believed that life moves in a circle from birth to death and they believed that circles in nature, such as the sun and moon, are important. Tribal councils sat in circles, and the tipi *(p.29)* was built into a circle, to acknowledge the importance of the shape.

What did Native Americans believe about nature?

Native Americans believed that everything in nature has a spirit, so it was important to respect nature and to live in harmony with it.

What roles did Native Americans have within the tribe?

People's roles within the tribe depended on age and gender.

- Women married, had children, looked after their families, owned and maintained the tipi *(p.29)*, and processed the buffalo *(p.28)*. They were highly respected for this vital role.
- Men hunted, and provided for their wives and children. They led the tribe and took part in tribal ceremonies. They were also in charge of fighting.
- The elderly were well looked after by their families. However, if they felt they had become a burden, they sometimes went away from the tribe voluntarily, to die from exposure.
- Children were held in very high regard and were rarely punished. They were expected to behave well and learn from their elders.

Why did Native Americans fight?

Native Americans fought other tribes for status or for hunting areas, or they raided others to steal horses. The Sioux were considered the most warlike of all the tribes.

How did Native Americans fight?

There were a number of main features of Native American warfare.

- Native Americans would attack and retreat, using ambush as the main fighting tactic. Brotherhoods took this on as their main role. They would only attack if they thought they would win. If they began to lose they would run away.
- Warriors demonstrated their bravery by 'counting coup' on someone from another tribe. A warrior had to attempt to touch an enemy with a coup stick, and then get away. The most skilled could do this without the enemy or himself being injured or killed.
- If a Native American killed another warrior, he could remove the top of his scalp and keep it as a trophy.

How were Native American tribes organised?

Tribes were organized in the folowing 5 ways.

- Each tribe was divided into 'bands' that worked together to survive.
- Each band could be as small as 20 or as large as several hundred people.
- Each summer, many bands might meet at a tribal gathering.
- Comanches met as a tribe a lot. Members could move between bands if they wished, as often as they wished.
- The Pawnee considered each band to be a separate village.

What was the biggest Native American tribe?

The Sioux was the largest tribe. It contained the sub-tribes of the Lakota, the Nakota and the Dakotas. The Lakota was so large it also had sub-tribes within it.

Who was the leader of a band in Native American tribes?

The most popular, most powerful and most successful members of a band were elected as the band's chief. A tribe could have lots of chiefs, each with a different role.

What were the different leaders of a band in the Native American tribes?

Depending on the needs of the tribe, they would have more or fewer chiefs. There were 3 popular types of leaders in a band.

- The War Chief.
- The Spiritual Chief.
- The Negotiation Chief, dealing with negotiations with other tribes.

How was the chief of a band chosen in the Native American tribes?

In Native American culture, reputation and power were typically gained with hunting or combat skills, and those who had gained a reputation could be chosen as chiefs.

What was the band chief's main responsibility in the Native American tribes?

A chief's main role was to make decisions for the band - usually on where they should move to, and where they should set up camp. Often the band had a council to make decisions, which was led by the chief.

What was the role of band elders in a Native American tribe?

Elders were wise people, who taught the culture and values in of the society to the younger members of the tribe, in order for their traditions and practices to continue.

What was the role of the band's council in Native American tribes?

The band's council would advise the chief in order to help him make decisions.

What are the names of some famous Native American chiefs?

Chiefs gained fame usually through wars with White Americans. Examples of famous chiefs are:

- Red Cloud *(p.38)*.
- Sitting Bull.
- Crazy Horse *(p.63)*.

What were brotherhoods in Native American culture?

Brotherhoods were an important part of Native American tribal culture.

- Brotherhoods were groups of men from the tribe or band. There could be many brotherhoods within the tribe or group.
- Members of brotherhoods taught the skills of warfare to the younger members of the tribe. They also helped with the buffalo *(p.28)* hunts.
- Men could only join a brotherhood if they had proven themselves brave and skillful warriors.
- Examples of brotherhoods in the Lakota Sioux included the Crow Owners, the White Horse *(p.28)* Riders, and the Strong Hearts.

DID YOU KNOW?

Native Americans made many great inventions. These included:

- ✔ Bunk beds.
- ✔ Chewing gum.
- ✔ Lacrosse.
- ✔ Kayaks.
- ✔ Toboggans.
- ✔ Hockey.

THE IMORTANCE OF HORSES

An animal used for its practicality, as well a symbol of status.

What was the importance of horses to Native American tribes?

Horses were essential to the Plains tribes, because they helped them move around and hunt buffalo *(p.28)*. Horses also demonstrated wealth and status.

How many horses might a Native American tribe have?

The number of horses a tribe had varied. They were a symbol of wealth, and were used as currency.

- In the 1870s, the Comanche had almost 8,000 horses, and 3,000 people.
- In the 1870s the Hunkpapa, one of the sub-tribes of the Sioux, had 3,500 horses and 2,900 people.

DID YOU KNOW?

There were no horses in America until the Spanish arrived in the 16th century.

The Pueblo Indians of Mexico captured the horses from the Spanish, and they were traded between tribes. It transformed their way of life and made hunting a lot easier.

THE IMPORTANCE OF THE BUFFALO

An animal that had range of different uses.

What is a buffalo?

A buffalo, or bison, is a large cow-like animal, native to North America.

Why were the buffalo important to the Native Americans?

The Native Americans relied on the buffalo to support their nomadic lifestyle in many ways. They were used for food, but also for clothes, utensils, and a multitude of other uses.

How did Plains Indians use the various parts of the buffalo?

There were many uses of the buffalo.

- Buffalo skin (or hide) was used for tipi *(p.29)* covers, shields, clothing, and shoes.
- The flesh of the buffalo was eaten.
- Buffalo fat was used for soap.
- Buffalo dung was used as fuel, and was smoked in ceremonies.
- Glue was made from the hooves of buffalo.
- Bowstrings were made from the sinews.
- The bones of buffalo were made into knives, jewellery, weapons, and toys.
- Buffalo horn was turned into cups and spoons.
- Buffalo tongue was used as a hairbrush.
- The fur of the buffalo was used for blankets, gloves, and padding for saddles.

Why did the buffalo almost become extinct?

After the Civil War, ex-soldiers and other white people went onto the Plains to shoot buffalo for sport. Numbers dropped so low that Native Americans could no longer sustain themselves, and were forced to live on reservations. By 1890 the buffalo had almost been hunted to extinction.

Why were the buffalo respected?

The many uses of the buffalo, combined with the Native American belief that all is sacred, meant that the buffalos were revered. This deep respect meant the Native Americans never wasted the buffalo, and used every part of them they could.

DID YOU KNOW?

The Natives Americans of the Plains took buffalo hunting very seriously.

- ✔ Before they went out on a hunt they would do a ceremonial 'Buffalo Dance', which sometimes lasted for days!
- ✔ It involved dressing as buffalos and mimicking their movement.
- ✔ It hoped to call on the spirit world to bring them good luck while hunting.

TIPIS

The homes of Great Plains tribes.

What is a tipi?

A tipi is a shelter that nomadic Native Americans lived in.

What were tipis made from?

A tipi was made from buffalo *(p.28)* hide, or skin.

Why did Plains Indians live in tipis?

Tipis were simple, which was important given the general lack of resources on the Plains. They helped the Plains Indians continue their nomadic lifestyle, as they were easy to put up, take down, and transport. They were also suited to the changeable weather on the Plains.

How were tipis suited to the Plains?

Tipis were conical, so harsh winds could blow around them. They had a flap for opening in the summer, to let cool air in. This could be closed in the winter, to keep warmth inside the tipi.

Who owned the tipis?

The women owned and maintained the tipi.

DID YOU KNOW?

The tipi was much more than a tent.

- ✓ Tipis were very practical: they could be taken down and transported very quickly, which made it ideal for the Native American tribes.
- ✓ It was the women who made the tipis, while the men decorated them with beautiful geometric patterns, and scenes of bravery shown in battles.

THE PERMANENT INDIAN FRONTIER

This created a boundary between the United States and Indian Territory.

What was the Permanent Indian Frontier?

The Permanent Indian Frontier was a border along the Mississippi River, dividing the eastern United States from what became known as 'Indian Territory'.

When was the Permanent Indian Frontier created?

The Permanent Indian Frontier existed from 1834.

DID YOU KNOW?

Indian territory got increasingly smaller, and eventually became the state of Oklahoma.

THE INDIAN TRADE AND INTERCOURSE ACT

An act to keep white settlers and Native Americans apart.

What was the Indian Trade and Intercourse Act?

The Indian Trade and Intercourse Act established the Permanent Indian Frontier *(p.30)*. It stated that all land west of the Mississippi River - but not in the states of Missouri, Louisiana or Arkansas - was 'Indian Territory'.

Why was the Indian Trade and Intercourse Act passed?

The Indian Trade and Intercourse Act was designed to keep white Americans and Native Americans apart.

How were white Americans affected by the Indian Trade and Intercourse Act?

The Indian Trade and Intercourse Act made it illegal for any white Americans to settle on the land west of the Indian Frontier. It also made it illegal to sell weapons or alcohol to the Native Americans.

How was the Indian Trade and Intercourse Act enforced?

To enforce the Indian Trade and Intercourse Act, white Americans built a military road and forts along the edge of the Indian Frontier. The forts were manned by the US Army.

DID YOU KNOW?

Native Americans were unable to leave their land without permission. This was another way in which they were controlled.

THE INDIAN REMOVAL ACT

An act which gave President Andrew Jackson complete control over the removal of Native American tribes to make room for white settlers.

What was the Indian Removal Act?

The Indian Removal Act brought Native Americans under the control of the United States. It forced those living east of the Mississippi River to move west beyond the Permanent Indian Frontier *(p.30)*, so they could live separate lives. This meant moving 46,000 Native Americans.

Who signed the Indian Removal Act?

President Jackson signed the Indian Removal Act.

When was the Indian Removal Act signed?

The Indian Removal Act was signed in 1830.

DID YOU KNOW?

Other than obvious opposition from Native American tribes to the Indian Removal Act, there was little opposition from white Americans. A small number of Christian missionaries opposed it.

THE TRAIL OF TEARS

The forced migration of tribes from the east, which resulted in horror and sadness.

What was the Trail of Tears?

The Trail of Tears was the forced removal of eastern tribes to land west of the Mississippi River in the 1830s, under the terms of the Indian Removal Act *(p.31)*. Many Native Americans died on the journey.

DID YOU KNOW?

The Trail of Tears remains one of many black marks in American History.

- ✔ What was done to the Native American peoples is very hard to understand.
- ✔ More than 100,000 Native Americans were forced to leave their homes. Before they embarked on the trail they were held in camps under the hot sun.
- ✔ Many underwent a journey of up to 1,000 miles.
- ✔ It has been estimated that more than 4,000 Cherokee died of starvation, exposure or disease. Many more from other tribes died on the journey.

THE FIRST INDIAN APPROPRIATIONS ACT

The beginning of reservations.

What was the First Indian Appropriations Act?

The American government passed the First Indian Appropriations Act to provide money to move Native Americans from the Indian Territory to reservations. It also allocated them land to hunt.

When was the first Indian Appropriations Act passed?

The Indian Appropriations Act was passed in 1851.

Why was the first Indian Appropriations Act passed?

The US Government wanted to move the Native Americans away from white settlers. The Act created reservations, to encourage Native Americans to abandon their nomadic lifestyle in favour of farming.

DID YOU KNOW?

The government hoped that Native Americans would turn to farming.

The Act reduced the amount of land there was for hunting buffalo. The government hoped that this would make Native Americans want to farm, and that they would adopt the ways of white Americans.

THE FIRST FORT LARAMIE TREATY

A treaty that gave some tribes a land and money, only if they let settlers cross the plains.

What was the Fort Laramie Treaty?

The Fort Laramie Treaty gave land and money to each Plains tribe if they let settlers, travellers, and government agents cross the Plains in safety.

Why was the Fort Laramie Treaty signed?

The US Government was under pressure to protect people migrating west, as the migrants were worried about conflict with the Native Americans. The Government's solution was to make an agreement with a council of different tribe leaders.

What problems were there in getting the Fort Laramie Treaty?

There were 5 main issues in arranging an agreement.

- The Council of Tribal Leaders. Gathering the leaders of each tribe was very problematic. Few tribes had an overall leader who could speak for all the bands within a tribe. Often the government chose them, which did not please the tribes.
- Inclusion. Many tribes were unrepresented. Some of those who attended the council only came for the food and gifts, and therefore did not take part in the discussions, to give their tribe's point of view.
- Boundaries. The US government wanted agreements made on borders and boundaries. However, Native Americans did not view land in this way. They saw land as there for everyone, and could not see why their movements needed to be limited.
- Language. Not all tribes spoke the same language, and there were not enough translators to make sure everyone understood the proceedings. Not all the tribes could engage properly with the negotiations.
- Attitudes. Some white Americans were exterminators, and did not believe a peaceful agreement could or should be reached. Some Native Americans, such as the Crow nation, felt the same.

When was the Fort Laramie Treaty signed?

The Fort Laramie Treaty was signed on 17th September 1851.

Who signed the Fort Laramie Treaty?

The Fort Laramie Treaty was agreed between the US government and Native American tribal chiefs.

What was agreed in the Fort Laramie Treaty?

There were 7 main points agreed in the Fort Laramie Treaty.

- Fighting would end between Native Americans and white Americans.
- Migrants could travel safely through Native American lands.
- Railroad surveyors would be allowed to enter Native American lands in safety.
- Road and army posts could be set up in the Native American lands.
- Native American tribes would have to pay compensation if they broke any of the agreement.
- The US Government agreed to protect Native Americans from white Americans, and to stop white Americans from settling on Native American lands.
- Native Americans were to receive an annual payment of $50,000, so long as they kept to the terms of the treaty.

How much money did the Fort Laramie Treaty give to the Native Americans?

The Native American tribes received $50,000 a year, as long as the treaty was unbroken. However some tribes never received payment.

What were the consequences of the Fort Laramie Treaty?

The Fort Laramie Treaty had 3 major consequences for the Plains Indians.

- It encouraged them to rely on the US government for food and money. This dependency also meant obedience.
- It gave each tribe their own land, rather than giving them the freedom *(p.52)* to be truly nomadic. This resulted in the creation of reservations.
- It ended the principle of the Permanent Indian Frontier *(p.30)*, as white Americans later settled in Native American lands, even though this broke the Fort Laramie Treaty.

DID YOU KNOW?

Many tribes were unaware of the true impact of letting settlers, government agents and travellers on their land.

- ✔ Grants from the government took away a lot the land from the tribes.
- ✔ It also left little space for the buffalo to graze, and there was nowhere for them to roam, which made hunting hard.

THE INDIAN WARS (1864-68): CAUSES AND CONSEQUENCES

Five years that changed many Native Americans' way of life, and saw them removed from their homelands and relocated. It was also a time of broken agreements by the US government, and the lives of many Native Americans were completely destroyed.

What were the Indian Wars?

The Indian Wars were a series of battles and massacres between Native American tribes, settlers, and government agents.

What caused the Indian Wars?

There were several reasons for the Indian Wars.

- Attitudes to land. The Native Americans didn't believe land could be owned, but laws such as the Homestead Act *(p.56)* encouraged settlers to rush onto the Plains to claim land. The belief in Manifest Destiny strengthened the settlers' belief that the land was theirs to cultivate.
- Attitudes to treaties. Native Americans within tribes didn't individually agree to the treaties made with the US government. Treaties were frequently broken as a result, as Native Americans strayed off their land.
- Poor conditions in the reservations. Native Americans were not treated well in many of the reservations. Food was often scarce, and the Native Americans starved to death on some reservations. This led to disagreements, which sometimes turned violent.
- Broken agreements. White settlers continued to cross Native American land, and even mined it. The government often did not pay compensation, which led to hostilities.
- Buffalo *(p.28)*. In the 1870s, the vast buffalo herds on the Plains were hunted almost to extinction by white hunters, who sold the hides but left the carcasses to rot. The grazing lands were also taken over by the cattle industry. The elimination of their main food supply brought the Sioux into armed conflict with the military.
- The introduction of the railroad. This displaced many Native Americans. It also disrupted the buffalo *(p.28)* herds.

What were the consequences of the Indian Wars?

There were 4 consequences of the Indian Wars.

- The American army destroyed Native American property and resources.

- The Native American population was reduced, due to starvation, fighting and disease.
- Relationships between the Native Americans and the settlers worsened.
- Native Americans were put onto smaller reservations, which had very poor quality land.

DID YOU KNOW?

One reason for the conflict was because of the belief that the Native Americans were inferior.

Many settlers and some in the US government felt justified in trying to get rid of the Native Americans: this can be seen in the case of the Sand Creek Massacre. The treatment of the Native Americans could be seen to be genocide, especially considering the total number of Native Americans deaths.

THE SIOUX WARS

A war between the Sioux tribe and the US government, which ended in devastating losses for the Sioux tribe.

What were the Sioux Wars?

The Sioux Wars is the name given to the ongoing conflict between the tribes of the Sioux and the US government.

When were the Sioux Wars?

The Sioux Wars began in 1854 at Fort Laramie, and ended in 1890 with the Wounded Knee Massacre.

LITTLE CROW'S WAR

Life was hard for the Dakota Sioux, and the land they were given did not live up to the promises of the government.

What was Little Crow's War?

Little Crow's War is the name of an attack by a band of Dakota Sioux, led by Little Crow, against the agency in charge of their reservation and white settlers in the surrounding area.

When was Little Crow's War?

Little Crow's War took place in August 1862.

Why did Little Crow's War happen?

The Dakota Sioux had been given inferior farm land by the government, which meant their crops failed. The government also failed to make agreed payments to the tribe, leaving them to starve.

What was the result of Little Crow's War?

700 white settlers and soldiers were killed by Little Crow's war band. As a result, the US Army sent soldiers to subdue the Sioux. 300 tribe members were sentenced to death, of whom 38 were hanged. The rest of the tribe was moved to the Crow Creek Reservation, where many starved. Any of them found outside the reservation were scalped for a bounty.

DID YOU KNOW?

Little Crow was eventually captured.

- ✓ Although Little Crow fled the scene he was found near Hutchinson, Minnesota, by a farmer. He was caught picking the farmer's raspberries, and was shot.
- ✓ The farmer got a $500 reward for Little Crow's scalp, which was put on display at the State Historical Society, Minnesota.

THE CHEYENNE UPRISING

An uprising that occurred out of desperation.

What was the Cheyenne Uprising?

Several Cheyenne groups faced starvation, because they had been given inferior reservation land in the Treaty of Fort Wise. They turned to attacking wagon trains, to steal food and other supplies.

When did the Cheyenne Uprising happen?

The Cheyenne Uprising took place in 1863.

DID YOU KNOW?

Before the uprising the Cheyenne had turned to eating grass to survive. The reservations agents showed no sympathy for their plight.

THE FORT WISE TREATY

US Congress declared that 'Indians should be treated as wards of the state.'

What was the Fort Wise Treaty?

The Fort Wise Treaty was an agreement between the US government and the Cheyenne and Arapaho tribes. The treaty gave the tribes' traditional hunting grounds to the US government, in exchange for $30,000 a year for 15 years, and reservation land in eastern Colorado.

When was the Fort Wise Treaty signed?

The Fort Wise Treaty was signed in 1861.

Why was the Fort Wise Treaty a problem?

Some of the Cheyenne and Arapaho felt they had not agreed to the treaty, so they did not follow its terms. They were called 'dog soldiers'.

> **DID YOU KNOW?**
>
> **Young warriors, known as the 'dog soldiers, rejected the treaty.**
>
> They refused to sign, and remained on the lands. Frequent skirmishes occurred between prospectors and the dog soldiers.

THE SAND CREEK MASSACRE

One of many unjustifiable killings of members of the Cheyenne and Arapaho tribes by US soldiers.

What was the Sand Creek Massacre?

The Sand Creek Massacre was the killing of over 150 Cheyenne and Arapaho by the US Army.

What was Black Kettle's role in the Sand Creek Massacre?

Black Kettle was one of the most important of the Cheyenne leaders. After the Cheyenne Rising he agreed to move his band onto a smaller reservation. They were camped at Sand Creek.

When was the Sand Creek Massacre?

The Sand Creek Massacre took place on 29th November 1864.

Where was the Sand Creek Massacre?

Sand Creek is in Colorado.

Why did the Sand Creek Massacre take place?

Black Kettle and his band of Cheyenne had moved to Sand Creek under instructions from the US authorities. Black Kettle was flying the white flag of truce on his tipi *(p.29)*. Colonel Chivington and his 700 cavalry made an unprovoked attack on the settlement.

What were the consequences of the Sand Creek Massacre?

Despite waving the white flag of surrender, 150 Cheyenne men, women and children were killed by the soldiers. Although he was initially praised, when the facts were known, Colonel Chivington was later forced to resign his post. A new treaty was made, and the tribes were moved to a larger reservation by the Arkansas River. Payments were promised to survivors of the massacre.

> **DID YOU KNOW?**
>
> **The Sand Creek Massacre was later described as 'the foulest and most unjustifiable crime in the annals of America.'**
>
> - ✓ It was seen as a murder of 150 women, children and men.
> - ✓ Chivington's men returned to Denver with scalps and other trophies, and were greeted and seen as heroic.
> - ✓ The real story came to light later.
> - ✓ There was inquest into the event, which condemned Chivington's actions. However, by this time he had left the army.

RED CLOUD'S WAR

After the government broke its treaty with the Sioux, the Sioux went on the attack.

What was Red Cloud's War?

Red Cloud's War was fought by the Sioux, Cheyenne and Arapaho tribes, against the US Army.

What role did Red Cloud have in the war?

Red Cloud led the Sioux against the US Army during Red Cloud's War. This included inflicting the Fetterman Massacre, which was the most serious defeat of the US Army until the Battle of the Little Bighorn.

When was Red Cloud's War?

Red Cloud's attacks lasted from 1866-1868.

Where was Red Cloud's War?

The attacks happened around the Bozeman Trail in Wyoming.

Why did Red Cloud's War happen?

In 1862 there was Gold Rush *(p.22)* in the Rocky Mountains. The Bozeman Trail was created, leading to new mining towns. Red Cloud believed it was an illegal road, which broke the Fort Laramie Treaty *(p.33)*. The Cheyenne and Arapaho had been moved to a smaller reservation than they had been promised.

What happened in Red Cloud's War?

The Sioux began attacking travellers on the Bozeman Trail. Peace talks took place, but when the US Army built forts along the Bozeman Trail to protect settlers, Red Cloud walked out. The Sioux then laid siege to the forts and attacked US soldiers. Sitting Bull and Crazy Horse *(p.63)* brought the Cheyenne and Arapaho into the war.

What were the consequences of Red Cloud's War?

The war ended with the Second Fort Laramie Treaty *(p.39)* in 1868.

- The US Army closed the forts on the Bozeman Trail.
- The Great Sioux Reservation was created.
- The Sioux agreed not to attack travellers, on the condition that no permanent white settlements were built on their land.

DID YOU KNOW?

Not all of the Lakota Sioux agreed with Red Cloud.

Some thought it was useless to fight the white settlers. They felt that, by signing the treaty, they would at least get something from the government.

FETTERMAN'S TRAP

A trap, orchestrated by a group of Native Americans, sprung on a troop of soldiers led by Captain Fetterman

What was Fetterman's Trap?

Fetterman's Trap, also known as the Fetterman Massacre, occurred during Red Cloud's War *(p.38)*. It was an attack by a group of Native Americans, on US soldiers led by Captain Fetterman.

When was Fetterman's Trap?

The soldiers were killed on 21st December 1866.

What happened at Fetterman's Trap?

A party of woodcutters was attacked, near Fort Phil Kearny, by a party of Sioux. As they had anticipated, a detachment of soldiers left the fort to protect the woodcutters. Many more Native Americans ambushed them and killed 81 soldiers, before blocking the route to the fort, rendering it unusable.

What were the consequences of Fetterman's Trap?

The Second Fort Laramie Treaty *(p.39)* was negotiated, which brought peace to the region for eight years.

DID YOU KNOW?

The Native Americans made sure the American soldiers were dead.

After the battle they stripped and scalped the American soldiers, then mutilated their bodies.

THE SECOND FORT LARAMIE TREATY

A treaty that guaranteed Arapaho, Dakota and Lakota tribes possession of some parts of the Dakota territory

What was the Second Fort Laramie Treaty?

The Second Fort Laramie Treaty was an agreement signed after the failure of the first Fort Laramie Treaty *(p.33)*. It was signed by the Lakota and Dakota Sioux, the Arapaho, and the US government.

When was the second Fort Laramie Treaty signed?

The treaty was signed in 1868.

What were the terms of the Second Fort Laramie Treaty?

The second Fort Laramie Treaty ensured peace between the Native Americans and the settlers. There were a number of terms to the treaty.

- The US Army closed the forts on the Bozeman Trail.
- The Great Sioux Reservation was created, which included the sacred Black Hills.

- The Sioux agreed not to attack travellers, on the condition that no permanent white settlements were built on their land.
- It gave the US government the authority to punish anyone who broke the treaty.

DID YOU KNOW?

The Government eventually broke the terms of the treaty.

When the Black Hills gold rush started, more and more white settlers moved into the sacred lands of the Sioux. The US government did nothing to stop them.

THE MISSOURI COMPROMISE

A compromise that put forward a balance of 'freedom'.

What was the Missouri Compromise?

The Missouri Compromise was an agreement that was signed when Missouri joined the United States.

When was the Missouri Compromise signed?

The Missouri Compromise was signed in 1820.

What were the consequences of the Missouri Compromise?

There were 2 key points in the Missouri Compromise.

- It said that there should be a balance of slave states and free *(p.52)* states as new states joined the Union.
- No new slave states were to be created in the North.

DID YOU KNOW?

The Compromise maintained the balance of power between pro-slavery states and anti-slavery states. This is why it was called a 'compromise'.

NAT TURNER'S REBELLION

A rebellion that scared many and strengthened the divide.

What was Nat Turner's Rebellion?

Nat Turner's Rebellion was a significant slave rebellion in the South, which caused widespread terror. Nat Turner and six other slaves stole property and killed 51 white people. It led to deeper tensions between slaveholders and abolitionists.

When did Nat Turner's Rebellion take place?

Nat Turner's Rebellion took place in 1831.

DID YOU KNOW?

After the rebellion Nat Turner hid for two months.

Once captured and put on trial he pleaded not guilty, as he was said in court that 'he was doing the work of God'. He was sentenced to death and hanged alongside others who were involved in the rebellion.

ABOLITION

A group of people that were against slavery and some would go to extreme means to end it.

Who were the abolitionists in the United States?

Abolitionists were groups of people - for example, the American Anti-Slavery Society - who campaigned for the abolition of slavery in the USA. They were more active in the northern states than in the southern ones.

When were the abolitionists active in the USA?

The abolition movement started in the eighteenth century. However, it gained traction from 1833, after the abolition of slavery in the British Empire. It ended after the emancipation *(p.52)* of slaves in 1865.

What did American abolitionists do?

The Anti-Slavery Society campaigned for abolition, and civil rights for ex-slaves. The society, and other organisations, helped the abolition debate enter American politics, and increased friction between northern and southern states.

THE COMPROMISE OF 1850

A temporary truce between those who argued about the issue of slavery

What was the Compromise of 1850?

The Compromise of 1850 dealt with new issues concerning slavery in the rapidly expanding United States.

What were the consequences of the Compromise of 1850?

The Compromise of 1850 included a number of key issues.

- It admitted California into the United States, and created the territory of Utah.
- It led to the passing of the Fugitive Slave Act *(p.42)*, and outlawed slavery in Washington DC.
- Local governments in the new south-west territories, rather than the federal government, could decide whether to allow slavery.

DID YOU KNOW?

It increased tensions between the North and South, and strengthened the anti-slavery movement.

THE FUGITIVE SLAVE ACT

A law which stopped slaves from gaining freedom.

What was the Fugitive Slave Act?

The Fugitive Slave Act was a law that said any escaped slaves should be returned to their masters.

When was the Fugitive Slave Act signed?

It was signed in 1850, as part of the Compromise of 1850 *(p.41)*.

DID YOU KNOW?

The 'Underground Railroad' helped many slaves gain freedom.

Harriet Tubman helped start the Underground Railroad, which helped over 100,000 slaves escape to the free northern states.

UNCLE TOM'S CABIN

'So you're the little woman who wrote the book that made this great war!'
Attributed to Abraham Lincoln when he met Harriet Beecher Stowe, the author of 'Uncle Tom's Cabin', in 1862.

What was 'Uncle Tom's Cabin'?

'Uncle Tom's Cabin' is a novel which tells the story of a slave, Uncle Tom. It was written to demonstrate the evils of slavery to Americans. The book was part of a wider abolitionist *(p.41)* movement before the Civil War, which encouraged people to see the evils of slavery.

Who wrote 'Uncle Tom's Cabin'?

'Uncle Tom's Cabin' was written by Harriet Beecher-Stowe.

When was 'Uncle Tom's Cabin' written?

'Uncle Tom's Cabin' was written in 1852.

DID YOU KNOW?

The book was as popular as the Bible.

It sold 300,000 copies in the USA, and was also very popular in Europe.

THE KANSAS-NEBRASKA ACT

A law which gave people in Kansas and Nebraska the choice over whether to be a 'slave state' or a 'free state'.

What was the Kansas-Nebraska Act?

The Kansas-Nebraska Act was a law which allowed people in those states to decide whether they wanted to introduce slavery.

When was the Kansas-Nebraska Act signed?

The Kansas-Nebraska Act was signed in 1854.

Why was the Kansas-Nebraska Act signed?

Kansas and Nebraska were created to allow the building of a northern transcontinental railroad *(p.60)*. Under the terms of the Missouri Compromise *(p.40)* they would become free *(p.52)* states. To gain the southerners' support for their creation, it was decided that they should make their own decision on whether to allow slavery.

What were the consequences of the Kansas-Nebraska Act?

There were a number of consequences of the Kansas-Nebraska Act.

- Tensions surrounding the issue of slavery grew, leading to 'Bleeding Kansas'.
- The Missouri Compromise *(p.40)* was now out of date as, in theory, new slave states could be created in the North.

DID YOU KNOW?

Border ruffians, pro-slavery settlers from the slave state of Missouri, helped contribute to pro-slavery laws and legislation.

Border ruffians crossed state borders to vote in Kansas on pro-slavery laws.

BLEEDING KANSAS

An increase in violence across Kansas, from 1854-1861.

What was Bleeding Kansas?

'Bleeding Kansas' is the name given to the outbreak of violence in Kansas, over whether the state would allow slavery for blacks under the Kansas-Nebraska Act *(p.43)*.

When was Bleeding Kansas?

'Bleeding Kansas' refers to the period in the state between 1854 and 1861.

What happened during the Bleeding Kansas period?

Two of the most famous events of 'Bleeding Kansas' occurred in 1856.

- The 'sacking of Lawrence' occurred when pro-slavery supporters entered the town and rioted, destroying anti-slavery newspaper offices.
- The Pottawatomie Creek Massacre occurred when John Brown, a radical abolitionist *(p.41)*, and his followers attacked the pro-slavery settlement, killing five people.

DID YOU KNOW?

Bloody clashes often occurred.

- There were violent clashes between pro-slavery and anti-slavery activists.
- One of the bloodiest events was when John Brown, an abolitionist, heard that an anti-slavery activist had been brutally attacked. He broke into the house of pro-slavery advocate John Doyle, and killed Doyle and his two sons.

THE HARPER'S FERRY RAID

An unsuccessful rebellion which heightened tensions.

What was Harper's Ferry Raid?

The Harper's Ferry Raid was the name given to the attack on a military store by abolitionist *(p.41)* John Brown and 18 other men, designed to instigate a slave rebellion.

When did the Harper's Ferry Raid happen?

The raid on Harper's Ferry took place in October 1859.

What were the events of Harper's Ferry Raid?

After Brown and his men captured the military store, it was surrounded and recaptured by US soldiers. 16 people were killed, and Brown was captured.

What were the consequences of the Harper's Ferry Raid?

There were 2 main consequences of the Harper's Ferry Raid.

- John Brown was tried and hanged.
- The incident heightened tensions between supporters of slavery and abolitionists, and led to even greater fear of slave revolts.

DID YOU KNOW?

Although the raid on Harper's Ferry was unsuccessful, Brown was seen as a martyr by abolitionists.

- Although the rebellion led to nothing, he was seen as a hero and is well remembered in American history.
- Alongside Brown, who was hanged, three of his sons were also killed.

ABRAHAM LINCOLN

A leader who implemented groundbreaking laws during his short presidency

Who was Abraham Lincoln?

Abraham Lincoln was the 16th President of the United States.

When was Abraham Lincoln president of the USA?

Abraham Lincoln was President of the United States of America from 1861 until his assassination in 1865.

Why is Abraham Lincoln important?

Abraham Lincoln was important to the Civil War in 2 main ways.

- As an anti-slavery president, he prompted southern states to secede from the Union after his election.
- In 1863 he issued the Emancipation *(p.52)* Proclamation, freeing all slaves in the Confederacy and allowing freed slaves to join the Union Army.

DID YOU KNOW?

Lincoln wasn't actually an abolitionist.

Although he aligned himself with them, and put forward the Civil Rights Law, he didn't want to interfere with states who wanted to keep slavery.

JEFFERSON DAVIS

A leader of a newly formed alliance.

Who was Jefferson Davis?

Jefferson Davis was the President of the Confederate States of America.

When was Davis president?

Jefferson Davis was the President of the Confederate States of America from 1861, until his capture at the end of the Civil War in 1865.

DID YOU KNOW?

Jefferson Davis was named after one of the Founding Fathers, Thomas Jefferson.

SECESSION

The first step of the Civil War.

What is secession?

The term 'secession' refers to the time when 11 states left the USA and formed the Confederate States of America (the Confederacy).

When did states secede from the USA?

South Carolina was the first state to secede from the United States of America in December 1860. It was followed by 10 others including Alabama, Florida, Georgia, Louisiana, Mississippi, and Texas.

Why did South Carolina and other states secede from the USA?

The election of Abraham Lincoln *(p.45)* as president in 1860 prompted the southern states to secede. As Lincoln was an opponent of slavery, the southern states felt he could not be trusted to maintain slavery.

DID YOU KNOW?

The day that South Carolina seceded led to celebrations and festivities across the state. There were fireworks, marching bands, and crowds of citizens flying the flag.

THE BATTLE OF FORT SUMTER

The trigger that started the American Civil War.

What was the Battle of Fort Sumter?

The Battle of Fort Sumter was an attack on Fort Sumter, by the South Carolina militia.

When was the Battle of Fort Sumter?

The Battle of Fort Sumter, which started the American Civil War *(p.47)*, was in April 1861.

DID YOU KNOW?

It wasn't the bloodiest of battles.

- ✓ Considering the number of artillery rounds that were fired, there were no casualties on either side.
- ✓ The only casualties were two soldiers who were killed during a 100 gun salute in the victory ceremony!

THE AMERICAN CIVIL WAR

A war between the Northern and Southern states, which had a devastating impact and changed the course of American History.

What was the American Civil War?

The American Civil War was an internal conflict between the northern and southern states of the USA.

When did the American Civil War happen?

The American Civil War was fought from 1861 to 1865.

Why was the American Civil War fought?

There were 5 main causes of the American Civil War.

- The debate around slavery meant that slave owners in the south disagreed with abolitionists in the north. The South wanted to keep slavery, because it provided plantation owners with a free *(p.52)* workforce.
- The nature of the US Government meant there was tension between states and the federal government about who had the right to make laws. The arguments often centered around slavery.
- Westward expansion meant that the issue of slavery was always discussed. New states were admitted to the Union, and it needed to be established whether they would be 'free *(p.52)*' states or 'slave' states.
- States that felt their liberty to make laws was being threatened said they would secede if they felt their views were not properly represented in Congress.
- There were economic differences. The climate in the South favoured agriculture, particularly cotton and tobacco growing. It was very profitable and relied on slave labour. However, the North was industrialised, and wasn't prepared to compete with slave labour.

What were the economic effects of the American Civil War?

There were 7 main economic effects of the American Civil War.

- The only real area of growth in both North and South was munitions production.
- The economy in the North was short of raw materials, as trade with the South was virtually eliminated.
- The economy in the South was inferior to that in the North, which had already industrialised. As a result the South was hit hardest, and couldn't adequately supply its army.
- Farms across the South were ruined by war, and crops and animals were confiscated. There were food riots later in the war, due to shortages.
- Cotton production in the South decreased dramatically. It also lost access to its European cotton markets, due to a naval blockade by the Union.
- Since the South had no real currency of its own, it suffered huge rates of inflation. Inflation was over 9,000% per year at its peak.
- The railroad system was severely damaged.

What were the social effects of the American Civil War?

There were several social effects of the American Civil War.

- Family life was disrupted for many Americans, who experienced conscription into the war effort.
- Since the North blockaded the South, people in the South suffered huge shortages of many things, including food and clothing.
- Many southerners found that their homes and properties had become part of a battleground, which created a large number of refugees.
- Some southern towns were placed under the control of the army (martial law), so people's rights were restricted.

- Since guerrilla warfare was common in the South, many southerners found they were living close to extreme and frightening violence.
- The war resulted in 600,000 dead and 400,000 wounded.

How were women affected by the American Civil War?

Thousands of women all over the United and Confederate states worked as nurses, or in the supply chains which supplied the troops with resources. Women also organised protests against appalling conditions, including an extreme lack of food, which led to starvation.

How did the American Civil War end?

The American Civil War ended in April 1865, when Robert E. Lee surrendered at Appomattox Courthouse in Virginia.

DID YOU KNOW?

The Union army was multicultural.

- The Union army (of the North) had soldiers from across Europe.
- In 1863 the Union army allowed black soldiers to serve; but they were not paid the same wage as their white colleagues.

THE MORMON WAR

A small conflict between the Mormons and the US government.

What was the Mormon War

The Mormon War (or Utah War) was a small scale war between the Mormons *(p.23)* and the US government. Most of its casualties were a result of the Mountain Meadows Massacre *(p.49)*.

When was the Mormon War?

The Mormon War was from 1857 to 1858.

What caused the Mormon War?

There were a number of causes of the Mormon War.

- There were growing tensions between Mormons *(p.23)* and pioneers travelling through Utah.
- Most Americans objected to the Mormons *(p.23)*' practice of polygamy.
- The US Government believed that Mormon leaders were running Utah along religious lines, supported by a paramilitary organisation called the Danites. It was felt that this undermined and obstructed the laws of the United States.
- President Buchanan wanted to replace Brigham Young *(p.23)* as governor of Utah with a non-Mormon governor. He sent 2,500 troops to Utah, to protect the new governor and prevent trouble.
- On hearing about the approaching army, Brigham Young *(p.23)* raised the local militia to defend Utah.

THE MOUNTAIN MEADOWS MASSACRE

A massacre that occurred because of the increasing tension against the Mormons and the US government.

What was the Mountain Meadows Massacre?

The Mountain Meadows Massacre was the killing of 120 travellers by the Mormon Danites.

When did the Mountain Meadows Massacre take place?

The Mountain Meadows Massacre happened on 7th September 1857.

Why did the Mountain Meadows Massacre happen?

The Mormons *(p.23)* were expecting an attack from the US Army. It is rumoured that the pioneer party that was attacked were taunting the Mormons. In this time of heightened unrest, the Danites attacked.

What were the consequences of the Mountain Meadows Massacre?

Danite leader John D. Lee was executed for his part in the murders. In 1858, an agreement was made with the US government about how Utah might follow laws in the wider US, and the Mormons *(p.23)* were pardoned. Finally, in 1896, Utah ended polygamy and was accepted into the Union.

DID YOU KNOW?

John D. Lee initially lied about what happened.

When captured, he blamed the killing on Indian tribes. When this was found to be untrue, he eventually admitted the truth.

RECONSTRUCTION

Bringing together the North and the South.

What was Reconstruction?

'Reconstruction' is the name given to the reunifying of the southern and northern states after the American Civil War *(p.47)*. It dealt with issues of emancipation *(p.52)* and the balance of federal and state power.

When did Reconstruction happen?

Reconstruction took place from the end of the Civil War in 1865, until its official end in 1877.

Who was in charge of Reconstruction?

Reconstruction was the responsibility of the federal and state governments. It was overseen by three presidents: Johnson, Grant, and Hayes.

What were the successes of reconstruction?

Reconstruction proved successful in several ways.

- Education became available to 600,000 black students.

- Infrastructure in the South that had been damaged during the war - such as railroads and bridges - was repaired and rebuilt.
- African Americans received equality under the law (although this was often in theory rather than practice).

What were the failures of reconstruction?

Reconstruction can be seen as a failure in some respects.

- Former slaves became trapped in debt through sharecropping.
- Reconstruction failed to change the racist attitudes of many white southerners. The Ku Klux Klan was formed at this time.
- By 1877, the federal government had moved on to dealing with other issues, such as the Sioux Wars *(p.35)*. As a consequence, old southern attitudes remained.

DID YOU KNOW?

To punish or not to punish?

Many wanted to harshly punish the South for wanting to leave the union in the first place, but both Lincoln and then Johnson were lenient towards the South after the Civil War.

PRESIDENTIAL RECONSTRUCTION

The first step of reconstruction.

What was Presidential Reconstruction?

'Presidential Reconstruction' is the term given to the first reconstruction *(p.49)* efforts led by President Andrew Johnson, in 1865 and 1866.

What happened during Presidential Reconstruction?

There were two main policies of Johnson's Presidential Reconstruction.

- It allowed the Southern states to return to the Union and manage their own affairs, in return for abolishing slavery and paying their war debts.
- It offered a pardon to southerners, except wealthy plantation owners and Confederate politicians, and the return of their property (excluding slaves).

What was the effect of Presidential Reconstruction?

Most Northerners initially supported Johnson's actions. However, the southern states used their powers to introduce the Black Codes, eroding support for Johnson in the North. Many Republicans wanted more radical policies to bring the southern states into line.

DID YOU KNOW?

Johnson grew up in poverty.

Johnson learned how to read at age 20.

RADICAL RECONSTRUCTION

Republican-led reconstruction.

What was Radical Reconstruction?

'Radical Reconstruction' is the term given to the period between 1866 and 1877, when the Republican Congress was in charge of Reconstruction *(p.49)* in the south. It led to the Reconstruction Acts.

DID YOU KNOW?

Radical Reconstruction wanted to go further.

Those who supported Radical Reconstruction wanted laws to go further to help the lives of black people.

THE RECONSTRUCTION ACTS

An effort to try and control the southern states.

What were the Reconstruction Acts?

The Reconstruction *(p.49)* Acts introduced new laws after the Civil War, during the Radical Reconstruction *(p.51)* period.

When were the Reconstruction Acts passed?

The Reconstruction *(p.49)* Acts were passed in 1867.

Why were the Reconstruction Acts introduced?

The Reconstruction *(p.49)* Acts were put in place to protect people and their property, and to help organise the South. It was an effort to impose the northern way of life on the people of the South, and eventually to bring the South back into the United States.

What new laws did the Reconstruction Acts introduce?

The Reconstruction *(p.49)* Acts included a number of measures.

- They put the army in charge of ten southern states, dividing the South into five districts, each under the control of the military.
- Southern states had to pass the Fourteenth Amendment *(p.53)* into law in order to rejoin the Union.
- They declared that all males, including African Americans, should be allowed to participate in the election of state governments.

DID YOU KNOW?

The full name of the Reconstruction Act was 'An Act to Provide for the More Efficient Government of the Rebel States'.

CARPETBAGGERS

Northerners were used to help the southern economy.

What were Carpetbaggers?

Carpetbaggers were northerners who moved South to gain employment. They helped to get the South back on its feet, but also took many high-ranking political jobs in Congress.

> **DID YOU KNOW?**
>
> **Carpetbaggers were many different types of people.**
>
> Originally they were ex-confederate soldiers. However, eventually, teachers, merchants and journalists also migrated to the South.

EMANCIPATION

It was a dawn of a new era for African Americans

What was emancipation?

'Emancipation' means to set free. After the Civil War, African Americans gained their legal freedom.

When were they emancipated?

African Americans were freed in 1865.

How was emancipation achieved?

African Americans gained their freedom in the Thirteenth Amendment *(p.53)*.

What was the impact of emancipation?

There were political, economic and social effects of emancipation.

- The southern economy was based on plantation farming using slaves. Banning slavery destroyed this way of life, because plantations couldn't operate without slaves.
- Poverty was a problem for white ex-slave owners as well as freed slaves, once the slaves had gained their freedom.
- Beliefs in white supremacy meant that black people were met with racism and violence in the South.
- Black people were elected into government for the first time in the history of the United States.
- Black people were given the right to vote when the Fifteenth Amendment *(p.54)* was passed in 1870.
- Many ex-slaves became refugees, and some moved north to look for work.

> **DID YOU KNOW?**
>
> **Many mark this as the start of the Civil Rights Movement.**
>
> Many see this as the beginning of the struggle for civil rights for African Americans, which was eventually achieved in 1964. However, even though the law was passed, the struggle is still ongoing.

THE 13TH AMENDMENT

'Neither slavery nor involuntary servitude ... shall exist within the United States.'
The 13th Amendment to the US Constitution.

What did the Thirteenth Amendment say?

The Thirteenth Amendment is the name given to the law that abolished slavery in the United States.

When was the Thirteenth Amendment signed?

The Thirteenth Amendment was signed in 1865.

DID YOU KNOW?

Although it made slavery illegal, life was still hard for African Americans.

The southern states put in place Black Codes, to stop African Americans from achieving civil rights.

THE CIVIL RIGHTS ACT, 1866

The granting of rights to those born in the United States.

What was the Civil Rights Act of 1866?

The Civil Rights Act of 1866 said that all people born in the United States were citizens with full legal rights. This became law as the Fourteenth Amendment *(p.53)*.

DID YOU KNOW?

These laws were not respected by all.

They caused a lot of uproar amongst many white Americans, especially in the South.

THE 14TH AMENDMENT

'Equal protection under the law.'
The promise made by the 14th Amendment to the US Constitution.

What did the Fourteenth Amendment say?

The Fourteenth Amendment is the name given to the law which gave equal rights and citizenship to African Americans after the Civil War. However, it did not guarantee them the right to vote.

When was the Fourteenth Amendment signed?

The Fourteenth Amendment was signed in 1868.

DID YOU KNOW?

Native Americans were not included.

Native Americans were only given full citizenship of the USA in 1924.

THE 15TH AMENDMENT

'The right of citizens of the United States to vote shall not be denied or abridged by the United States or by any State on account of race, color, or previous condition of servitude.'
The 15th Amendment to the US Constitution.

What did the Fifteenth Amendment say?

The Fifteenth Amendment gave all American citizens the right to vote. It ensured no one could be denied the vote due to their former status as a slave, or due to their race. However, southern states got around this by making it difficult for African Americans to vote - for example, by making voters pass literacy tests.

When was the Fifteenth Amendment signed?

The Fifteenth Amendment was signed in 1870.

DID YOU KNOW?

It barely made a difference to the rights of African Americans.

The southern states made up new ways to stop African Americans from voting, such as implementing impossible-to-pass literacy tests, and raising the poll-tax for African Americans.

THE CIVIL RIGHTS ACT, 1870

A law that tried to protect the voting rights of Black Americans.

What was the Civil Rights Act of 1870?

The Civil Rights Act of 1870 (also known as the Enforcement Act) underlined the Fifteenth Amendment *(p.54)*, by explaining the right of the federal government to prosecute anyone stopping African Americans from voting.

How did the Civil Rights Act of 1870 support the 15th Amendment?

The Civil Rights Act supported the 15th Amendment in two key ways.

- It made it illegal to discriminate in voting on the basis of race or colour.
- It made it illegal to wear disguises, threaten violence, or intimidate officials during the voting process.

Why was the Civil Rights Act of 1870 passed?

The Civil Rights Act (1870) was introduced because white southerners opposed equality for African Americans. For example, the Ku Klux Klan was formed in 1865, in Tennessee, to promote white supremacy and to terrorise African Americans.

DID YOU KNOW?

It was also known as the Emancipation Act of 1870.

THE BLACK CODES

These laws took away the freedom that African Americans had been granted.

What were the Black Codes?

The Black Codes were a series of local laws which restricted the new freedoms of African Americans. They varied from state to state, but had the goal of keeping ex-slaves under the control of white people.

What sort of freedoms were restricted under the Black Codes?

The Black Codes differed by area, but typically they banned marriage between blacks and whites, stopped African Americans from testifying in court, and limited their ownership of property.

When were the Black Codes passed?

The Black Codes were enacted from 1866, and were in place for decades.

DID YOU KNOW?

These laws allowed for African Americans to be discriminated against, and ensured that they held little if any power.

African Americans were expected to follow specific rules that only applied to them. For example, in Mississippi they had to make sure that, each January, they had written evidence of employment. If they could not produce it they were arrested.

THE FREEDMEN'S BUREAU

An organisation set up to help those at the lower end of society.

What was the Freedmen's Bureau?

The Freedmen's Bureau was a government agency set up to help freed slaves and very poor white people in the South. It gave them legal assistance, as well as helping with education, housing and food.

DID YOU KNOW?

Its main achievement was setting up schools to provide education for former slaves.

The act gave 90,000 African Americans an education.

SHARECROPPERS

An opportunity that seemed like freedom, but often wasn't.

What were sharecroppers?

Sharecroppers were former slaves turned farmers. The landowner supplied housing and tools, while the sharecroppers grew the crops and were allowed to keep a share of what they produced. They were not treated well by their white employers, and were always in debt.

DID YOU KNOW?

Sharecropping was, in effect, just another term for slavery.

Sharecroppers did not have great way of life. They were often still in poverty, and often found themselves deeply in debt to the landowners.

THE HOMESTEAD ACT

An opportunity for white settlers to have a better chance at life.

What was the Homestead Act?

The Homestead Act was a law, signed by Lincoln, which gave farmers 160 acres of Plains land (called a homestead). The land was free *(p.52)* so long as it was successfully farmed for five years. It cost just $10 to register and claim this land.

When did the Homestead Act become law?

The Homestead Act was signed into law in 1862.

How was land distributed before the Homestead Act?

Before the Homestead Act the government owned all the land in the West, then sold land at $1 an acre. This was too expensive for most people to afford.

Who could claim land using the Homestead Act?

To file a claim you needed to be over 21 years old (unless you were an ex-soldier), and either single or the head of a family. This opened up claiming to more people: those in the process of becoming a US citizen, ex-slaves, and women. Native Americans were still excluded.

What were the rules to the Homestead Act?

To prevent business owners snapping up land and making a profit from it there were strict rules. A person could not file numerous claims. They had to live on the land, build a house, plant at least five acres of crops, and work it for five years.

What was 'proving up' under the Homestead Act?

If the rules were followed for 5 years the homestead could be bought out fully for $30. This was called 'proving up'.

What did the Homestead Act achieve?

As a result of the Homestead Act, over 6 million acres of government land and over 80 million acres of public land were settled. Nebraska's population grew so much that it became a state in 1867.

How did the Homestead Act help migration?

The Homestead Act encouraged people to migrate to the West, who would not have been able to do so before. Nebraska alone was boosted by 123,000 immigrants - almost half the population of the state.

What were the problems with the Homestead Act?

There were 5 main limitations to the Homestead Act.

- Proving up was not common, so much of the land stayed as homesteads. By 1900 only 24 million acres had been proved up; and, overall, 60% of the land was never proved up.
- Although a lot of land was given over to homesteads, more land went to the railroads (300 million acres), and to cattle ranchers, who paid highly for it.
- Many homesteaders bought their land from the railroad companies, instead of through the government scheme.
- Rich landowners sometimes abused the scheme by getting employees to claim land as a homesteader *(p.58)*, then handing the rights over to the landowner.
- Part of the scheme allowed people to pay $1.25 an acre for land, which they were allowed to sell after six months of living there and ploughing at least an acre of it. They could earn profits using the scheme.

DID YOU KNOW?

There were certain requirements to get free land.

In order to get the land, you had to be over 21 and the head of the household.

THE TIMBER CULTURE ACT

More land given to homesteaders in order to plant trees.

What was the Timber Culture Act?

The Timber Culture Act was a law which gave homesteaders 160 acres of land in addition to that permitted by the Homestead Act *(p.56)*, so long as they planted 40 acres of it with trees.

When was the Timber Culture Act signed?

The Timber Culture Act was signed in 1873.

Why was the Timber Culture Act important?

Trees were extremely important in the West. They could be used as a barrier to the strong winds; houses could be built from it; and it could be burnt as a fuel. However, there were few trees on the Great Plains, so timber was rare, and expensive to bring to the Plains. The Timber Culture Act was designed to encourage the planting of trees.

What were the problems with the Timber Culture Act ?

Many trees died, as they did not have enough water. Also, people used the Act to claim more land, which they sold for a profit after a few years.

What were the successes of the Timber Culture Act?

In Minnesota large numbers of trees were planted successfully.

DID YOU KNOW?

Trees were an important way of life.

They provided fuel, and could be used to build houses.

THE DESERT LAND ACT

Free land given to settlers.

What was the Desert Land Act?

The Desert Land Act gave settlers, for free *(p.52)*, 640 acres of poor quality land which needed to be irrigated.

When was the Desert Land Act signed?

The Desert Land Act was signed in 1877.

DID YOU KNOW?

You didn't actually have to live on the land.

This led to many companies using people to make false claims.

HOMESTEADERS

Land was available to settlers, who had enough savings, to maintain the land.

What was a homesteader?

A homesteader was a farmer who accepted land under the Homestead Act *(p.56)*.

Why did homesteaders move west?

There were 3 main reasons why there was a rise in the number of people moving west after the Civil War.

- The US Government introduced new laws to encourage settlement of the west.
- The construction of transcontinental railroads made it easier to travel west and to transport supplies there.
- Many ex-soldiers and ex-slaves wanted to start a new life after the Civil War.

What problems did the homesteaders experience?

Homesteaders had a number of challenges when trying to farm the Plains.

- There was a lack of materials for building homes and fences.
- There was a lack of fuel for fires and cooking.
- There was a lack of water from rivers and rainfall.
- The weather could be unpredictable and dangerous.
- The soil was tough, and difficult to plough.
- There was a problem with pests. Crops could be trampled by buffalo *(p.28)*, or eaten by swarms of grasshoppers.
- Many of the crops that homesteaders farmed, such as maize, did not grow well on the Plains.
- Homesteads were spread out, so there was a lack of a close community for social interaction, goods and services.

How did the homesteaders solve their problems?

While many homesteaders' attempts to farm failed, some did discover solutions to the problems. A number of new ideas and inventions helped make life easier for the homesteaders.

- Sod, or tough mud, was dug up and used to build houses.
- Barbed wire was invented by Joseph Glidden in 1874, which made it possible for homesteaders to fence their land.
- Homesteaders used buffalo *(p.28)* chips (dried buffalo dung) as fuel.
- In 1854, Daniel Halladay invented a windmill that helped to pump underground water to the surface.
- Farmers used 'dry farming' methods to keep moisture in the soil.
- In 1830, John Deere made the 'sodbuster' plough, which could cope with the tough earth on the Plains.
- New machinery, such as threshers and reapers, were developed. Large areas of land were particularly suited to mechanisation.
- Russian settlers on the Plains brought new, hardy varieties of crop, such as Turkey Red wheat.
- As the railroads developed, supplies were brought to the homesteaders on the Plains. It also meant they could travel more easily.

DID YOU KNOW?

Land was purchased, then resold to European immigrants.

Promises of a better life were publicised in newspapers in England, Holland and Germany.

TRANSCONTINENTAL RAILROADS

Impressive railroads which connected east to west.

What were transcontinental railroads?

Transcontinental railroads were the railways which linked eastern USA to the western states.

When were the transcontinental railroads built?

The first transcontinental railroad, the Union-Pacific, was built between 1863 and 1869. Another four were constructed by 1900.

Where did the transcontinental railroads start and end?

The first transcontinental railroad ran between Omaha, Nebraska, and Sacramento in California.

What were the problems with the transcontinental railroad?

There were 5 main problems with the construction of the transcontinental railroad.

- The railroad was costly, and it was difficult to raise money for its construction.
- The railroad had to navigate difficult terrain, including mountains and deserts.
- Hostile Native Americans attacked railroad workers.
- It was difficult to find enough people willing to work on the railroads.
- The living and working conditions were terrible.

Why were transcontinental railroads so important?

Transcontinental railroads were important because they helped people move onto the Great Plains and travel across the United States. Railroad companies offered cheap land next to the tracks, which helped more people settle on the plains.

What impact did the transcontinental railroad have on settlers and farmers?

The railroad had several effects on settlers and farmers:

- Travel became significantly cheaper and more convenient.
- Towns and businesses grew rapidly around the railroad as it brought in more people.
- Transporting goods became easier and cheaper. This meant farmers could make more money by selling their grain further away.
- More products were brought to settlers: machinery, household items and luxuries became more widely available.
- Many immigrants from Europe were able to settle with great success.

What impact did the transcontinental railroad have on Native Americans?

The railroad had several effects on Native Americans.

- The railroad routes and tracks encroached even more on their lands, forcing them to move away.
- To try and prevent railroads being built they attacked railroad surveyors. This led to conflict with the US Army.
- The railroad caused a further reduction in buffalo *(p.28)* numbers as it reduced the grassland they needed for food. It also brought in hunters, who killed great numbers of buffalo.
- Some tribes, including the Pawnee, Omaha and Winnebago, signed treaties with the US government and moved on reservations.

What impact did the transcontinental railroad have on the USA?

The railroad had a significant impact on the USA as a whole.

- The railroad boosted the economy. As it connected east and west, trade became easier and quicker. It also opened Asia up to American markets.
- Many Americans felt Manifest Destiny had been achieved, and America was now becoming a united nation.

What impact did the transcontinental railroad have on the homesteaders?

The railroad had 3 main effects on homesteaders.

- Transport was faster and easier, making it simpler to visit friends and family.
- Homesteaders could bring in goods to make their lives easier. They could order goods from the east using mail order, such as from the Sears, Roebuck & Company catalogue.
- Towns grew rapidly around the railroad, which allowed communities to form. Homesteaders could discuss farming ideas, socialise, and sell and buy products.

DID YOU KNOW?

The Union-Pacific railroad was 1,776 miles long.

THE RESERVATION SYSTEM

Reservations were set up in order for white settlers to take over Native American land.

What is a reservation?

A reservation is a fenced off area of land, where the Native Americans were forced to live in order to make way for westward expansion.

What was life like on the reservations?

Life on the majority of reservations was hard, and the Native Americans were often neglected by those who were supposed to care for them. Native Americans were expected to live life as white Americans did, ignoring their own culture and heritage. If they refused, rations were stopped.

Why did the Native Americans move to the reservations?

There were several reasons why the Native Americans agreed to move onto reservations.

- The US Government made it sound as if the move was to protect them, and that they would be looked after.
- Many tribes were struggling to survive, as a result of having less land, less food, and more disease.
- They thought that moving to the reservations would mean that they could continue their way of life and customs in peace.

What happened if the Native Americans did not want to move to the reservations?

If the Native Americans tribes refused to move to the reservations, they were forced by the US Army.

Why did the US government want the reservations?

The US government wanted to try and separate the Native Americans and white Americans. They hoped this would reduce the tensions between them. They also wanted to try and 'Americanise' the Native Americans, converting them to Christianity and teaching them to become farmers.

What problems came from the reservations?

The reservations caused many problems for the Native Americans.

- Chiefs often agreed to treaties which they could not enforce on their tribes, as they did not have the authority to do so.
- Some reservations were situated far from sacred places that the Native Americans wanted to visit.
- Some rival tribes were placed together on the same reservations, which caused its own issues. For example, the Apache and the Navajo were placed together.
- The land in the reservations was often poor quality, even for those who did attempt to farm. This meant that the Native Americans were even more dependent on the government for supplies.
- The Bureau of Indian Affairs managed the reservations, but their officials were often corrupt.
- The government often reduced the size of the reservations after pressure from white Americans, who said that it was unfair that the Native Americans had so much land.

DID YOU KNOW?

Life on a reservation was difficult.

The Native Americans on the reservations suffered problems of infant mortality, low life expectancy, poor nutrition, poverty, and alcohol and drug abuse.

THE MEDICINE LODGE TREATY

'You give us presents and then take our lands; that produces war.'
Buffalo Chip of the Cheyenne.

What was the Medicine Lodge Treaty?

The Medicine Lodge Treaty ended the large reservation system, and moved the Native Americans of the Southern Plains onto smaller reservations in Oklahoma. It ensured that the Native Americans stayed on the reservations and adapted their way of life to that of white Americans.

When was the Medicine Lodge Treaty signed?

The Medicine Lodge Treaty was signed in 1867.

DID YOU KNOW?

It was initially seen as a peaceful treaty.

It was signed by many tribe leaders, despite hostility from native chiefs. However, in the years after it was signed, Congress sought ways to break the rules of the treaty.

THE SECOND INDIAN APPROPRIATIONS ACT

An extension of the first Indian Appropriations Act.

What was the Second Indian Appropriations Act?

The second Indian Appropriations Act took power away from individual tribes, and brought all Native Americans under US law as 'wards' of the US government.

When was the Second Indian Appropriations Act signed?

The second Indian Appropriations Act was signed in 1871.

DID YOU KNOW?

The Indian Appropriations Act was, essentially, a way to steal more land.

The act made it a lot easier for the US government to steal land from the Native Americans and to issue it to white settlers.

CRAZY HORSE

A determined man who fought for his tribe's rights.

Who was Crazy Horse?

Crazy Horse was a famous Sioux leader, who fought for his tribe's right to move freely on the land. He led the Oglala Sioux at the Battle of the Little Bighorn. He surrendered to the US Army in 1877, and was killed while resisting imprisonment later that year.

SITTING BULL

A brave chief who managed to gain many victories for his people.

Who was Sitting Bull?

Sitting Bull was a Sioux leader, who united his men against the US Army. He led the Lakota Sioux and Northern Cheyenne during the Battle of the Little Bighorn. He was killed by reservation police officers in 1890.

GENERAL CUSTER

A highly regarded general who had big ambitions

Who was George Armstrong Custer?

George Armstrong Custer was a United States Army officer. He served as a cavalry commander in the American Civil War *(p.47)* and the American Indian Wars.

What was George Armstrong Custer's role in the Indian Wars?

After the American Civil War *(p.47)* he pursued US aims in the West, and participated in a campaign against the Sioux and Cheyenne Indians. He spent the next few years in many skirmishes with the Plains Indians, and developed the view that they were savages.

What was George Armstrong Custer's Black Hills expedition?

Custer led the Black Hills expedition for the United States Army. Its mission was to look for suitable locations for a fort, to find a route to the southwest, and to investigate the possibility of mining for gold. Gold was found in the Black Hills, which prompted a gold rush *(p.22)*. This, in turn, antagonised the Sioux, as their sacred land had been protected by treaties with the US government.

What did George Armstrong Custer do in the Battle of Little Bighorn?

Custer led the 7th Cavalry in a disastrous attack against the largest gathering of Plains Indians ever seen. He was killed at the Battle of the Little Bighorn, in what became known as 'Custer's Last Stand.'.

What legacy did George Armstrong Custer leave?

Custer was given a hero's burial at West Point. Owing to his status as a Civil War hero, his death shocked the American people. As Americans came to regret their government's mistreatment of Native Americans, however, Custer's image changed.

DID YOU KNOW?

Custer used cinnamon oil on his hair.

- ✓ Custer took his looks very seriously, and wore elaborate uniforms.
- ✓ He used cinnamon oil on his hair, to make his blond locks glossy.

THE BATTLE OF THE LITTLE BIGHORN

A victory for the North Plains Indians, which ultimately led to their defeat.

What was the Battle of Little Bighorn?

The Battle of the Little Bighorn took place at the Little Bighorn River, in Montana Territory.

Who fought in the Battle of the Little Bighorn?

The Battle of the Little Bighorn was fought between an alliance of Sioux, Cheyenne and some Arapaho, against the US Federal Army commanded by George Armstrong Custer *(p.64)*.

When was the Battle of the Little Bighorn?

The Battle of the Little Bighorn took place on 25th and 26th June, 1876.

What were the causes of the Battle of Little Bighorn?

There were 4 main reasons for the Battle of the Little Bighorn.

- In 1875, gold was discovered in the Black Hills of South Dakota. This led to an influx of gold miners, which broke the Second Fort Laramie Treaty *(p.39)*. The US Government did nothing to stop the prospectors.
- The US Government offered to buy the Black Hills from the Sioux. As this was sacred land, the Sioux refused.
- In December 1875, Sioux and Cheyenne people refused an order from the US Government to return to their reservations. Instead, they joined Sitting Bull and Crazy Horse *(p.63)* in Montana.
- Some Sioux began attacking the miners and other settlers. The US Army was sent to the area to protect the settlers, and to force the Sioux and Cheyenne back to their reservations.

What happened at the Battle of the Little Bighorn?

There were several key events at the Battle of the Little Bighorn.

- On 25th June, Custer discovered a Sioux village. He also spotted a nearby group of around forty warriors, and attacked them before they could alert the main party. However, Custer was unaware that the warriors in the village vastly outnumbered his force.
- The Sioux and Cheyenne crossed the river together, meeting the advancing soldiers and forcing them back. At the same time another force, commanded by Crazy Horse *(p.63)*, surrounded Custer and his men. They began the attack with heavy gun- and arrow-fire.
- As the Native Americans closed in on Custer, he ordered his men to shoot their horses, and stack their bodies up to form a protective barrier. This, however, did little to protect his troops from the enemy bullets.
- Custer and his men were killed in less than an hour. It was the worst military disaster America had seen.

Why was Custer defeated at the Battle of the Little Bighorn?

There were 9 key reasons for the defeat of Custer at the Battle of the Little Bighorn.

- Custer was arrogant and over-confident. He wanted a victory to bolster his political ambitions (as he was considering running for president).
- Even though he was told to wait for support, Custer ignored orders and acted alone.
- Custer force-marched his men through the mountains, instead of going around them. By the time he arrived, his troops and their horses were exhausted.
- Custer divided his force into three groups. Although this was a standard US Army tactic, it weakened his already outnumbered force.
- Custer did not know how big the Sioux army was, or how well armed the warriors were. He had poor and incorrect information.
- He was vastly outnumbered. There were up to 1,500 Sioux warriors against around 250 US troops.
- He expected the Sioux to scatter and run. Instead, they outmanoeuvred and surrounded him.
- Crazy Horse *(p.63)* and other Sioux leaders were talented and experienced commanders.
- The Sioux fought with determination and desperation, as they regarded the battle as their last chance to defeat the US.

Why was the Battle of Little Bighorn important?

Little Bighorn showed the Native Americans' power: they had achieved their greatest victory. However, outraged over the death of a popular Civil War leader, the US government fought back.

What were the consequences of the Battle of the Little Bighorn?

Despite their victory, the Battle of Little Bighorn had 5 main consequences for the Sioux nations and Plains Indians as a whole.

- Once news spread that more than 250 US soldiers had been killed by the Sioux, public opinion quickly turned against the Native Americans.
- Plains Indians had to stay on their reservations. Any found outside their reservations were pursued by the army and killed. By the early 1880s, almost all Cheyenne and Sioux were confined to reservations, totally dependent on the US government for food and shelter.
- Previous treaties were now ignored. The government decided that Native Americans had forfeited the rights to have any special treatment, and started to eliminate Native American culture.
- The Sioux were forced to sell the Black Hills, and their reservations were split up.
- To prevent any future Sioux attacks their weapons and horses were taken. New forts were built, and the number of soldiers in the area increased.

DID YOU KNOW?

No-one knows what happened to Custer's body, although there have been different rumours.

- Some say he was scalped.
- Others say that his body was ripped apart, and that his ear drums were pierced because he had refused to listen to the Native Americans.

THE DAWES ACT

The Dawes Act provided a way to give white settlers more land.

What was the Dawes Act?

The Dawes Act was a law which distributed Indian reservation land to individual Native American families. They were given a plot of land, with the intention that they would become self-sufficient farmers.

Who authorised the Dawes Act?

President Grover Cleveland authorised the confiscation and redistribution of Native American lands.

When did the Dawes Act become law?

The Dawes Act was enacted in February 1887.

Why was the Dawes Act created?

The objective of the act was to:

- Further encourage Native Americans to integrate into white American society.
- Free *(p.52)* up more land for white settlers.

What were the effects of the Dawes Act?

The Dawes Act helped to further destroy Native American culture.

- It undermined the tribal structure of Native Americans, as they were now citizens of the USA.

- It eliminated the need to hunt buffalo *(p.28)*.
- It eroded Native American spiritual beliefs, which were often focused on their culture and tribal structure. Some Native Americans became Christians.

DID YOU KNOW?

The provisions of the Dawes Act were only available to some Native American tribes.

They were not available to Cherokee, Creek, Choctaw, Chickasaw, Seminole, Miami, Peoria, the Osage, Sac, and Fox in the Oklahoma Territory. Nor were they available to the reservations occupied by Seneca Nation of New York. The list goes on!

THE GHOST DANCE

A way for the Native Americans to regain what had been taken from them.

What was the Ghost Dance?

The Ghost Dance was a new religious movement among the Native Americans, which incorporated many of their traditional beliefs.

When did the Ghost Dance begin?

The Ghost Dance began on January 1st 1889, during a solar eclipse.

Who started the Ghost Dance?

The Ghost Dance was started by a Native American holy man called Wovoka.

Why did Native Americans do the Ghost Dance?

Many Native Americans believed they had angered the gods by abandoning their culture, which had caused their misfortunes and defeat. They practised the Ghost Dance as a way of making amends, in the hope that the gods would create a new world for them.

What did Native Americans believe about the Ghost Dance?

Native Americans believed that the Ghost Dance religion would do 4 main things.

- It would bring an end to white settlement in America.
- The buffalo *(p.28)* would return.
- Their ancestors would come back to life.
- Their traditional way of life would be restored.

What were the consequences of the Ghost Dance?

The Ghost Dance worried the US Government, who tried to ban the religion. This led to the 'Ghost Dance War', which ended at Wounded Knee.

DID YOU KNOW?

Many hoped that the Ghost Dance would banish the European settlers.

- ✓ The practice of the Ghost Dance spread throughout the west, even up to the Canadian border.
- ✓ The Native Americans hoped to get their land back, and also that the buffalo (which had been hunted almost to extinction) would return.

WOUNDED KNEE

The final battle between Sioux Indians and the US Army. Its significance lives on today.

What was the Wounded Knee Massacre?

The Battle of Wounded Knee (or the Wounded Knee Massacre) was the final battle in the wars between the US Army and the Sioux.

Who was involved in the Battle of Wounded Knee?

The Battle of Wounded Knee was between the Sioux Indians, led by 'Big Foot', and the 7th US Cavalry.

When was the Battle of Wounded Knee?

The Battle of Wounded Knee happened on the 29th December 1890.

Where did the Battle of Wounded Knee take place?

The Battle of Wounded Knee took place at Wounded Knee Creek on the Lakota Pine Ridge Indian Reservation, in the US state of South Dakota.

What happened at the Battle of Wounded Knee?

The US Cavalry were sent to disarm the Sioux and arrest their leader, Big Foot. One of them resisted, and the soldiers opened fire. Over 250 Sioux and 25 troopers were killed.

DID YOU KNOW?

Wounded Knee began as a scuffle, when the firing of one shot led to a massacre.

- ✓ The US soldiers opened fire on Sioux Indians, shooting as many men, woman and children as possible.
- ✓ The massacre lives on in the memory of Native Americans of all tribes.
- ✓ There was no inquiry into what happened - in fact, the soldiers were given medals, and the public expressed approval of the way they had conducted themselves.

THE OKLAHOMA LAND RUSH

Settlers rushed to take up land in the newly opened Oklahoma territory. The land was cheap and plentiful.

What was the Oklahoma Rush?

At the end of the Plains Wars, the western territories became states of the USA. The government opened up these new lands for settlement. The first area was Oklahoma, and the land grab there became known as the Oklahoma Land Rush.

Who was involved in the Oklahoma Land Rush?

White settlers were allowed onto this section of land by the US government, making Oklahoma available for homestead claims. White settlers rushed in, and took land from the Native Americans.

Where did the Oklahoma Land Rush happen?

The land that was opened to settlement for the white settlers included all or part of Cleveland, Kingfisher, Logan, and Oklahoma.

When was Oklahoma Land Rush?

The Oklahoma Land Rush began on the 22nd April 1889, in Central Oklahoma, USA.

Why was the Oklahoma Land Rush significant?

The Oklahoma Land Rush was significant as another example of how the US government gave away Native American land, due to pressure and demands from white settlers.

DID YOU KNOW?

Oklahoma was originally land set aside for Indians.

- ✓ Many tribes, such as the Apache and Cherokee, had been relocated to Oklahoma.
- ✓ However, with improved ranching and agricultural techniques, white settlers were attracted to Oklahoma - it was cheap to relocate, but the land could become very valuable.

THE CLOSURE OF THE FRONTIER

A danger for Native Americans, but a chance of freedom for the settlers.

What was the closure of the frontier?

In 1890, the US Census Bureau closed the frontier. The West had been fully settled so the frontier had, in effect, ceased to exist.

What was the impact of the closure of the frontier?

There were 3 main consequences of the frontier closure.

- The preservation of wild areas, which later resulted in national parks such as Yellowstone and Yosemite.
- Manifest Destiny had, officially, been achieved.

- The frontier had represented danger because of the Native Americans who lived in the region. This was no longer the case.

DID YOU KNOW?

The closing of the frontier was seen as a very significant event in American history.

At the time it offered many European settlers an opportunity to start a new life. However, it had a detrimental impact on Native Americans: the forced migration to reservations, the impact of the wars, and many deaths from European diseases.

A

Abolish, Abolished - to stop something, or get rid of it.

Abolition - the act of abolishing something, i.e. to stop or get rid of it.

Agriculture - an umbrella term to do with farming, growing crops or raising animals.

Alliance - a union between groups or countries that benefits each member.

Assassination - the act of murdering someone, usually an important person.

B

Blasphemy - the act of speaking insultingly about or with lack of reverence for God or sacred objects.

C

Campaign - a political movement to get something changed; in military terms, it refers to a series of operations to achieve a goal.

Carpetbagger - the name given to someone from the northern states of the USA who moved south after the American Civil War to help with reconstruction efforts. The term comes from the bags they often carried which were made from carpet.

Casualties - people who have been injured or killed, such as during a war, accident or catastrophe.

Cavalry - the name given to soldiers who fight on horseback.

Civil rights - the rights a citizen has to political or social freedoms, such as the right to vote or freedom of speech.

Conscription - mandatory enlistment of people into a state service, usually the military.

Corrupt - when someone is willing to act dishonestly for their own personal gain.

Council - an advisory or administrative body set up to manage the affairs of a place or organisation. The Council of the League of Nations contained the organisation's most powerful members.

Coup - a sudden, violent and illegal overthrow of the government by a small group - for example, the chiefs of an army.

Culture - the ideas, customs, and social behaviour of a particular people or society.

Currency - an umbrella term for any form of legal tender, but most commonly referring to money.

D

Danites - a Mormon militia group.

Debt - when something, usually money, is owed by a person, organisation or institution to another.

Disarm - to remove any land, sea and air weaponry.

Discriminate, Discrimination - to treat a person or group of people differently and in an unfair way.

E

Economic - relating to the economy; also used when justifying something in terms of profitability.

Economy - a country, state or region's position in terms of production and consumption of goods and services, and the supply of money.

Emancipation - liberation through gaining economic, political and social rights.

Export - to transport goods for sale to another country.

Extreme - furthest from the centre or any given point. If someone holds extreme views, they are not moderate and are considered radical.

F

Fasting - to deliberately refrain from eating, and often drinking, for a period of time.

Fatalities, Fatality - Deaths.

Federal - in US politics this means 'national', referring to the whole country rather than any individual state.

Frontier - a line or border between two areas.

G

Guerrilla tactics, Guerrilla warfare - a way of fighting that typically involves hit-and-run style tactics.

I

Immigrant - someone who moves to another country.

Independence, Independent - to be free of control, often meaning by another country, allowing the people of a nation the ability to govern themselves.

Industrialisation, Industrialise, Industrialised - the process of developing industry in a country or region where previously there was little or none.

Industry - the part of the economy concerned with turning raw materials into into manufactured goods, for example making furniture from wood.

Inflation - the general increase in the prices of goods which means money does not buy as much as it used to.

Infrastructure - the basic physical and organisational facilities a society or country needs to function, such as transport networks, communications and power.

Integrate - to bring people or groups with specific characteristics or needs into equal participation with others; to merge one thing with another to form a single entity.

M

Manifest destiny - the belief white Americans had the God-given right to expand westwards across North America.

Massacre - the deliberate and brutal slaughter of many people.

Mechanisation - Where human workers are replaced by machines or robots.

Militia - an army created from the general population.

New World - the name given in the 16th century to describe the Americas and the Caribbean, distinguishing it from the 'Old World', which referred to Europe.

Paramilitary - a group of unofficial or private soldiers organised along military lines.

Persecution - hostility towards or harassment of someone, usually due to their race, religion or political beliefs.

Pioneer - the first person to explore or settle in a new area.

Polygamy - the practise of being married to more than one person at the same time.

Population - the number of people who live in a specified place.

Poverty - the state of being extremely poor.

President - the elected head of state of a republic.

Prevent, Preventative, Preventive - steps taken to stop something from happening.

Printing press - a machine that reproduces writing and images by using ink on paper, making many identical copies.

Production - a term used to describe how much of something is made, for example saying a factory has a high production rate.

Profit - generally refers to financial gain; the amount of money made after deducting buying, operating or production costs.

Prosecute - to institute or conduct legal proceedings against a person or organisation.

Prospector - someone who searches for gold.

Radical, Radicalism - people who want complete or extensive change, usually politically or socially.

Raid - a quick surprise attack on the enemy.

Rebellion - armed resistance against a government or leader, or resistance to other authority or control.

Reconstruction - a period in the USA from 1865-1877 where the southern states were reintegrated through a series of laws.

Refugee, Refugees - a person who has been forced to leave where they live due to war, disaster or persecution.

Reservation - an area of land given to Native Americans by the US government to keep them away from settlers.

Riots - violent disturbances involving a crowd of people.

Secede, Secession - formal withdrawal from a larger entity, such as 11 states leaving the United States prior to the American Civil War.

Sharecropper - someone who farmed land belonging to a landowner in return for giving them a share of their crops.

Siege - action by enemy forces to surround a place or building, cutting off access and supplies, with the aim of either destroying it, gaining entry, or starving the inhabitants out.

Sod - the surface of the ground, often mud, on which grass is growing.

State, States - an area of land or a territory ruled by one government.

Tactic - a strategy or method of achieving a goal.

Terrain - a stretch of land and usually used to refer to its physica features, eg mountainous, jungle etc.

Territories, Territory - an area of land under the control of a rule country.

Treaty - a formal agreement, signed and ratified by two or more parties.

Ward, Wards - A ward is someone who is taken under the protection and power of someone else, usually because it is believed that they do not have the capacity to know what is best for them.

Lightning Source UK Ltd.
Milton Keynes UK
UKHW051049090921
390261UK00003B/71